For our families,

Hanna, Noah, and Joe
Jasper, Jonas, and Ed

for their love and patience.

Contents

Weaving Through Words

Using the Arts to Teach Reading Comprehension Strategies

ROBERTA D. MANTIONE
Boulder Community School of Integrated Studies
Boulder, Colorado, USA

SABINE SMEAD
Boulder Community School of Integrated Studies
Boulder, Colorado, USA

INTERNATIONAL
Reading Association
800 BARKSDALE ROAD, PO BOX 8139
NEWARK, DE 19714-8139, USA
www.reading.org

Director of Publications   Joan M. Irwin
Editorial Director, Books and Special Projects   Matthew W. Baker
Senior Editor, Books and Special Projects   Tori M. Bachman
Production Editor   Shannon Benner
Permissions Editor   Janet S. Parrack
Acquisitions and Communications Coordinator   Corinne M. Mooney
Assistant Editor   Charlene M. Nichols
Administrative Assistant   Michele Jester
Editorial Assistant   Tyanna L. Collins
Production Department Manager   Iona Sauscermen
Supervisor, Electronic Publishing   Anette Schütz
Senior Electronic Publishing Specialist   Cheryl J. Strum
Electronic Publishing Specialist   R. Lynn Harrison
Proofreader   Elizabeth C. Hunt

Project Editor   Corinne M. Mooney

Cover   Design, Linda Steere
         Art, Laurel Schiavone-Lambert, age 9

Library of Congress Cataloging-in-Publication Data
Mantione, Roberta D.
    Weaving through words : using the arts to teach reading comprehension strategies / Roberta D. Mantione, Sabine Smead.
        p.   cm.
Includes bibliographical references (p. 191) and index.
    ISBN 0-87207-456-0
1. Reading comprehension—Study and teaching (Elementary).   2. Arts—Study and teaching (Elementary).   3. Interdisciplinary approach in education.   I. Smead, Sabine.   II. Title.
    LB1573.7 .M28 2002
    372.47—dc21

                                                                    2002013255

Preface

All over the United States, reading comprehension is a hot topic. In our educational community in Colorado, teachers and staff developers have been engaged in an inquiry into how to relate the extensive research on reading comprehension to teaching practice. Staff developers from the Denver-based Public Education and Business Coalition (PEBC) have been working in local schools to share with teachers ways to implement innovative strategies for teaching comprehension. Books written by PEBC staff, such as Debbie Miller's *Reading With Meaning: Teaching Comprehension in the Primary Grades* (2002), show how to use these strategies in the classroom. Ellin Keene and Susan Zimmermann's *Mosaic of Thought: Teaching Comprehension in a Reader's Workshop* (1997) is a classic book on the topic of reading comprehension. Stephanie Harvey and Anne Goudvis's *Strategies That Work: Teaching Comprehension to Enhance Understanding* (2000) also provides ideas for practical applications of reading comprehension strategies in the classroom.

Our school, the Boulder Community School of Integrated Studies (BCSIS), provides a unique environment in a public school setting. At BCSIS, parents, teachers, local artists, community members, international guests, and children work together to nurture and honor artists of every age and to blend artistic endeavor with an academic approach that supports multiple intelligences (for more on the theory of multiple intelligences, see chapter 1). The mission of our school is twofold: (1) to develop an aesthetic sensibility and (2) to create a new paradigm of education that uses the arts to enhance intellectual development. Ultimately, the school's desire is for children and adults to work as artists in their pursuit of knowledge. Understanding and respect for the world community is fostered through engaging in art forms of many cultures.

A unique characteristic of our school is that teachers stay with a group of students for more than one year. So during the course of writing this book, all BCSIS teachers taught three different grades. Sabine, for example, taught second, third, and fourth grade during this time.

Our school is a focus school that operates as a magnet school. It attracts a diverse group of students from the city and county. Approximately 15% of the student body is comprised of children who are African American, Native American, Hispanic American, or Asian American. Seventeen percent of the children in the school are in special education. About 12% of BCSIS students receive free or reduced lunches.

At BCSIS, teachers and parents work together to paint the walls of the classrooms and hang curtains in the windows. Students play the recorder each morning, and the smell of baking bread drifts from the kindergarten class. On walks, students gather natural materials in woven baskets found at garage sales. Teachers create aesthetic classrooms to please the eye and to encourage spontaneous creation and imaginative problem solving, with the overall effect of creating a community that values the arts. They make a commitment to maintain a print-rich environment without becoming overstimulating.

A number of years ago, the state of Colorado introduced the Colorado Basic Literacy Act, which states that all students need to be at grade level in reading by third grade. One of the outcomes of this act was that our district enhanced our staffing with the addition of a literacy specialist. At BCSIS, Roberta moved from the classroom into this position, which enabled her to work closely with Sabine and her second-grade class. The high number of these second graders who were nonreaders challenged us. Many of these students also had nontraditional learning styles: We observed children who were primarily kinesthetic learners and other children who had difficulty processing information. In order to reach these students and help them become competent readers, we knew we had to do some intensive work. We also knew we had to develop a wider repertoire for teaching reading comprehension strategies.

During this time, we observed a fourth-grade book club in a workshop sponsored by PEBC. The students in this book club were learning how to use reading comprehension strategies to build meaning from the text they were reading. We watched the students use sticky notes to mark passages in which they had questions. We listened to them share aloud their inferences with the group, and we were impressed by their ability to analyze text. After observing these students, we wanted to teach the children in our school the same reading comprehension strategies, specifically

- developing sensory images,
- building and activating schema,
- questioning,

- determining importance,
- inferring, and
- synthesis.

Keene and Zimmermann (1997) have identified and synthesized these strategies as the thinking processes that strategic readers bring to a text to develop meaning. Because of our school's premise that learning is about creating meaning in the world, we believed that comprehension should be the backbone of a balanced reading program.

Furthermore, because we are an arts focus school, we asked ourselves, "How can the arts help children figure out the things they don't understand?" and "Do the arts have some quality that actually helps children think, learn, and stay engaged?" This then led us to the question, "Can we use the arts to teach reading comprehension strategies?" We wondered if using an arts approach would afford children the opportunity to infuse a variety of visual, kinesthetic, and musical activities into their attempts to use these reading comprehension strategies to gain meaning from text. We knew from our experience of integrating the arts into science and social studies that the arts increased children's learning power. Research summarized in *Champions of Change: The Impact of the Arts on Learning* shows that "students involved in the arts are doing better in schools than those who are not—for whatever constellation of reasons" (Catterall, Chapleau, & Iwanaga, 2000, p. 4). One reason this may occur is that "the arts serve to broaden access to meaning by offering ways of thinking and ways of representation consistent with the spectrum of intelligences scattered unevenly across our population" (Catterall et al., p. 4). In our case, we wanted to meet the intelligences of the students in Sabine's class, and eventually, in all classes in our school.

We saw clear connections between the type of thinking in which children engage while doing art and while using the thinking strategies they need to become literate. The arts not only nurture an authentic commitment and passion for learning, but they also develop these thinking strategies. According to David Perkins (1994), "Although we think of the arts as primarily a visual phenomenon, looking at art thoughtfully recruits many kinds and styles of cognition—visual processing, analytical thinking, posing questions, testing hypotheses, verbal reasoning and more" (p. 5). We made a deliberate decision to use the arts to teach reading comprehension strategies. By including a broad range of artistic disciplines in our approach—painting, drawing, music, movement and dance, construction and architecture, storytelling, and poetry and drama—children could experience using their imaginations, creative thinking, aesthetic sense, and artistic skills in multiple ways.

Our aim for this project was to work with all students and teachers in our school in order to explore using the arts to teach reading comprehension strategies to a wide range of ages and classes. However, some classes were more involved in the project than other classes. We usually introduced a strategy through the arts approach to the whole class, and often, this would encompass more than one arts lesson. Roberta, as the literary specialist, used the same arts approach with small groups of struggling readers and gifted students and with student-selected interest groups in the class to expand their use of the strategy. Over time, most whole- or small-group reading comprehension instruction in Sabine's class had become embedded in the arts. As other teachers invited us to work with their students, we worked collaboratively with teachers in their classrooms. This collaboration enabled us to gain instant feedback about the lesson. The progress in our work was subtle at first, but as we became more excited about students' learning, we began to share more about our project with other teachers and administrators. And students brought home their excitement about these lessons and shared it with their parents. The support and enthusiasm we received for this three-year project was based mainly on witnessing students' growth in reading, thinking, and passion for learning.

Weaving a Tapestry of Comprehension

Strong comprehension comes from weaving the intellectual, emotional, and multisensory components of thinking. We wanted a curriculum and classroom environment that engaged each student's head, hands, and heart because the only way to have critical and creative thinking is to have students use all aspects of their cognitive beings. We drew our goals from witnessing the profound effect that the arts have on children's interactions in the world and with books. We, then, had the following goals for children's learning:

- To use the arts to help students deepen their comprehension of text
- To engage students in comprehension activities that match their strongest intelligence
- To explore how students' natural play in the arts could extend to comprehension

- To expose students to a multisensory/multiple sign system approach to learning and understanding (for specifics on the multiple sign system approach, see chapter 1)
- To increase students' intellectual passion

In addition, we had the following goals for ourselves:

- To understand more about how the arts help children's cognitive growth
- To broaden our teaching repertoire
- To use the arts to teach reading comprehension

Through these goals, we envisioned creating a curriculum for comprehension that was similar to weaving an intricate tapestry. Just like in weaving, in which the manner you lay the warp, or foundation, will determine the patterns and richness that emerge, the components of our arts curriculum laid the foundation for students' ability to comprehend text. And so we launched our project of integrating the arts with the teaching of reading comprehension.

The first time we used the arts to teach a comprehension strategy felt like taking a plunge from the high dive. There were so many unknowns; we wondered if the students would become engaged in literacy or would experience this lesson as just a fun activity. Could we expect them to really transfer what they had learned about the arts to their comprehension of text, or would this learning sit in isolation? Perhaps the biggest unknown was, Could we really develop meaningful lessons on an ongoing basis, or would developing these art lessons become too cumbersome?

So we started off with small steps, teaching the strategies with which we were most comfortable and using the art mediums we loved. Our first lesson was about the strategy of questioning, and we had students look at numerous pieces of art and write down their questions. However, as we began to feel more confident teaching the strategies and saw how motivated the students were, it became easier to think of more complex ways of integrating the arts. We found that ideas for art lessons came to us in surprising ways, such as spending time in bookstores browsing through oversized art books or skimming the pages of a children's biography of a famous artist. A more formal approach for developing these lessons was the art walk, as suggested by Julia Cameron in *The Artist's Way: A Spiritual Path to Higher Creativity* (1992). This approach is when you make a date with yourself—whether it is a trip to a museum, an interesting shop, a nature area, or the inside of another school during halftime at a basketball game—and notice the artwork and beauty in the immediate environment. Often, an art walk inspires rich connections to your teaching.

What we found most surprising during our project was that even when using the arts in limited ways, students were responsive and enthusiastic. Indeed, their energy and passion brought out new excitement in our teaching. Other teachers with whom we worked during this project have taken a stronger interest in using the arts—some have taken slow, cautious steps like us, whereas others have just taken the plunge. We hope the ideas and lessons in this book help you see the connection between the arts and reading comprehension. More important, we hope this book offers you some support in using the arts in your literacy teaching. We trust the arts will nourish you and your students, just as the arts have nourished us and our students.

Ultimately, we hope to share with you an approach to teaching reading comprehension that reaches a broader range of students. We know that in order for students to comprehend what they read in a lasting, meaningful way, they need to engage in text in an interactive manner. We found that the arts provided tools that helped us have a greater effect on our students' learning. This was not an expensive project, and we are not art specialists. The fact that art can be integrated with all areas of curriculum enables everyone to use the arts to enhance students' learning. The arts offer many possibilities that are simple, powerful, and accessible to all. This book will help you find new, innovative ways to teach the critical strategies of reading comprehension to your elementary grade students. You can easily adapt the lessons in this book for middle school students, as well.

Organization of This Book

Chapter 1 shows how the arts work to build students' comprehension and cognitive abilities in reading and introduces the six strategies of reading comprehension—developing sensory images, building and activating schema, questioning, determining importance, inferring, and synthesis—that guide the overall structure of this book. We are grateful for the ongoing work of Keene and Zimmermann (1997) and Harvey and Goudvis (2000), and this chapter explains how instrumental their work has been in our arts approach to teaching comprehension. This chapter also looks at various research on comprehension and the arts, as well as how the arts affect learning.

We have organized and labeled chapters 2–7 according to the reading comprehension strategies. Each chapter begins with a brief explanation of the strategy being discussed and why the arts are useful in teaching the strategy. The chapter then shares an in-depth arts lesson that incorporates that strategy. This section assesses how the arts affected the learning of the strategy, as well as the students' comprehension throughout the lesson. Finally, the chapter provides six art-based lessons, for a variety of grade levels, that teach the strategy. Interspersed throughout these chapters are students' artwork and writing samples that provide evidence of students' growing ability to comprehend text.

Chapter 8 examines individual case studies of students with special needs and shows how the arts helped these students achieve higher levels of reading comprehension.

Chapter 9 shares numerous assessments we used to gauge students' learning. We summarize some of the students' growth in their passion for the arts and in their ability to use the reading comprehension strategies to gain meaning from text. We also briefly review students' scores on state and district achievement tests.

The chapters are followed by an epilogue, as well as four appendixes. Appendix A provides an arts matrix that will support you in implementing the art lessons described throughout the book. Appendix B shares techniques for specific art projects and drama. Appendix C offers blackline masters of assessment forms discussed in chapter 9. Appendix D provides resources for books, websites, and art suppliers.

This book encourages you to embrace your creative energies and the arts from the world around you in order to add a new dimension to your literacy teaching. We want to inspire you to bring art into your life and the lives of the children you teach. We learn more each day from the children with whom we work, as well as the many people who have gone before us and developed the current body of knowledge around cognition, the arts, and reading comprehension. We hope this book helps you do the same.

Acknowledgments

Writing this book with the students and staff at BCSIS has been delightful. We are grateful for the friendship and willingness of the teachers who worked with us, listened to us, and let us in their classrooms—Jan, Erin, Suzanne,

Batya, Diane, David, Sara, Katie, Becca, and Kara. Our working relationship with Rosie Waters, director of the Imagination Makers Theater Company, provided dynamic conversations about the role of drama in learning. Special thanks to our principal, Betsey, who created a learning environment that encourages teachers to take risks and grow. The heart of this project was the work with the students. A special thanks goes to Sabine's class, who worked so closely with us during the project. They were eager, adventurous, and supportive every step of the way. After every project, they were willing to dissect the work and share their thinking. Without them, this book would never have become a reality.

We are grateful for all the people in our lives who were willing to read various drafts, give us feedback, and laugh about our lack of subject-verb agreement. We cherish their friendship and value their input. There were many people who joined us around the kitchen table for intense dialogue that stretched our thinking. These conversations sustained us. We would like to acknowledge a few people who gave us a great deal of their time—Patricia, Rodrigo, Jeannie, Jacki, Ari, Cathy, Judy, Phil, Andy, Anna, Julie, Jim, Barbara, Susan, Steve, Mary, Ed, and Marla.

We appreciate the vision of Matt Baker and Corinne Mooney at the International Reading Association. Their hard work in guiding us through the various manifestations of this manuscript has helped bring out the essence of our work.

Finally, we thank our families for their belief in us and encouragement of our work and our dreams. Thanks to Simone, Susan, Tom, Gail, Bonnie, Barbara, Dave, and our parents, Vera, Ray, and Borka, for teaching us to be passionate about life.

RDM and SS

Chapter 1

Integrating Reading Comprehension and the Arts

The arts add the kind of richness and depth to learning and instruction that is critical to healthy development.

—Judith Burton, Robert Horowitz, & Hal Abeles, 2000, p. 36

A few days into the school year, we notice mysterious activities on the playground at all three recesses: Students from the second-grade class begin gathering at the one shady spot on the playground, hidden behind the back corner of the building. Initially, about eight children collect in this spot, looking like a disorganized reunion of old friends. By the second day, however, things become more complex: Students have papers and pencils in hand and begin writing, and a few students canvass classrooms to borrow musical instruments to take outside.

By the end of the week, the whole second grade is meeting at their designated shady spot. Boys sit in the corner knitting; other students play chimes, drums, and *shekares* (African rattles); and two girls stand up front, like orchestra conductors, trying to corral this mass of creative energy.

We spend time each recess watching them through the classroom window, using the curtain as a cover. We are getting a glimpse into the creative process of this group and are awestruck at the coordination and cooperation that are unfolding.

One afternoon, at the last recess of the day, Sierra and Tegan come running into the class. They announce that their play is ready, and they would like a few minutes to perform it for us. The rest of the ensemble enters the room: Six boys get their knitting bags and sit in the corner, the narrators march to the center of the "stage," a group of students starts to play their instruments, and three girls grab their backpacks and run into the other room to change into their costumes. Then, the play begins. The parents of a young fairy princess who had fallen ill are frantically looking all over the kingdom to find a cure. Each time the narrator speaks, the chimes sound to mark the narrator's lines. The play moves from scene to scene, directed by Sierra, who has to stop the action every so often to remind people where they are supposed to be.

At the end of the play, students are eager to share how the play unfolded and take credit for what had been done. It turns out that

Sierra and Tegan are the playwrights and that they had asked who would like to join them and had accepted everyone. Sierra says they eventually ran out of parts, so they decided that the six boys who were latecomers could sit and knit for the queen.

Upon reflection, we realized that this production had not happened in isolation. In the few weeks since school began, the second graders had been immersed in the study of drama and literature. They had been creating and performing small plays in small reading groups, in shared reading, and while performing music. For these students, drama was a rich and direct method to express the stories they wanted to learn and share. The dramas they had performed in class had been so motivating that the students were extending these literacy experiences outside the classroom.

Witnessing this drama take shape sparked a passionate dialogue between us about the power of drama to capture students' imaginations. The central question we kept returning to was, "How can we use students' creative thinking and passion about books, stories, and drama to teach them reading comprehension strategies they can use as tools for meeting the demands of understanding more difficult text?"

The arts require everyone to interact with their whole selves, thereby engendering the intellectual passion we so dearly want for all children. Teaching reading comprehension strategies through the arts is an approach that is an inclusive, multidimensional, passionate experience. Through this experience, students gain a broad and complex understanding of reading comprehension and reading comprehension strategies, which they can use for lifelong learning. Weaving the arts through a study of comprehension helps build a stronger fabric of understanding.

What Is Reading Comprehension?

We define reading comprehension as the interactive thinking process in which a reader engages while reading text that enables his or her understanding to develop. In the classroom, *comprehension* means that students are able to make sense of what they read. Teachers know students comprehend when they are able to ask reflective questions or provide insightful comments while making connections between the text and their own lives. Students show their ability to comprehend text by making inferences and defending their decisions and viewpoints. Strong comprehension allows readers to solve problems with text and apply text to real-life situations. Ultimately, comprehension is an individual's ability to construct meaning as he or she reads.

What Are the Reading Comprehension Strategies?

As previously noted, teachers in our school use *Mosaic of Thought: Teaching Comprehension in a Reader's Workshop* (Keene & Zimmermann, 1997) and *Strategies That Work: Teaching Comprehension to Enhance Understanding* (Harvey & Goudvis, 2000) to guide their instruction. These books have laid a strong foundation by detailing the philosophy, reasoning, and lesson planning for teaching reading comprehension strategies. These strategies are not a step-by-step process, such as underlining the topic sentence, but rather reflections of authentic thought processes that weave together to develop meaning. The following sections define and explain the six strategies of reading comprehension, as set forth by Keene and Zimmermann.

Developing Sensory Images

Sensory imagery is one of the most powerful tools readers bring to a book. When readers build images as they read, they assimilate details, organize thoughts, make comparisons, visualize, and develop personalized movies of the text in their minds. All these processes allow readers to remember and access what they have read, which is the basis of reading comprehension.

Building and Activating Schema

The process of building schema for a new text means that readers must focus on paying attention to the rich connections between their lives and the text so they can create deeper meanings from the text. Although this process may include teaching students the meaning of challenging vocabulary or supplying them with background information, it also includes creating experiences that help children build foundations for new understandings of text. These understandings can take the form of text-to-self, text-to-text, or text-to-world connections. For example, in a story about a cat, children might say how the story reminded them of their cats (text-to-self connection), the cat in another book they have read (text-to-text connection), or perhaps the cat in a recent newspaper article (text-to-world connection).

Questioning

Questioning is the act of asking, probing, and wondering. As a reading comprehension strategy, questioning helps spark readers' imaginations and engages them in the story. Questioning allows readers to self-monitor their comprehension and moves them through a piece of writing. By asking questions, readers are pursuing the unknowns of a story.

Determining Importance

This strategy helps readers determine the essentials of text. Readers learn to distinguish between interesting details of a text and the primary message, or the author's message. During the reading of nonfiction, determining importance is the strategy that helps readers sort out the critical information for research and learning.

Inferring

Inferring never happens in isolation because it weaves the reader's prior knowledge, text connections, questions, and predictions and the author's information and summaries into a personal tapestry of understanding. To infer requires readers to move beyond the obvious but remain focused on the text. It also requires that readers use their perspectives of the world to clarify and gain meaning from the text. Through this strategy, readers develop unique, personal understandings of text.

Synthesis

Synthesis is the ability to use all the other strategies—developing sensory images, building and activating schema, questioning, determining importance, and inferring—in order to organize and summarize a text while adding the dimension of personal meaning. As previously noted, these strategies have been identified by research as the thinking processes that strategic readers bring to a text to develop meaning (Keene & Zimmermann, 1997). Once students use these strategies fluently, they have tools to help them interact effectively with the text. We now recognize that meaningful comprehension relies on the reader having an active, personal interaction with the text.

Why Use the Arts to Teach Reading Comprehension Strategies?

We told the women in our book group about our project of integrating arts and reading comprehension and asked them how they interacted with books when they were children. Memories came pouring out. One woman told us, "I was Laura Ingalls Wilder for three Halloweens in a row. My whole backyard was the prairie, and we played out each one of the books." Another woman said, "After reading *Harriet the Spy* (Fitzhugh, 1964), I went out and bought a journal and started taking notes about everything." We realized that when they were children, these women lived books but did not talk about books. The transformation from reading a book to becoming the book's characters seems to be children's self-selected answer to the adult world of book groups, although "Jean Piaget, through his clinical research on children's thought processes, has made us acutely aware that children are not 'miniature adults'" (Cecil & Lauritzen, 1994, p. 3).

Although adults often dismiss this as only child's play, we have observed that when children act out a story, paint a picture of a character, or write a song, they actually are developing strategic thinking. Through arts activities, we have watched students take on the viewpoints of multiple characters in a story, deal with complex layers of plot development, and explore the ambiguity of a text. It seemed to us that students wanted to take a more active, creative, multisensory response to the books they were reading. The theories and research discussed in the following sections demonstrate how we endeavored to provide students with the tools that would allow them to respond to text in more complex ways.

Multiple Intelligences

A strong impetus for using the arts to teach reading comprehension strategies is that they engage students in multifaceted experiences. And as Howard Gardner demonstrates in *Frames of Mind: The Theory of Multiple Intelligences* (1983), all people have a variety of intelligences. Gardner describes an approach to understanding intelligences that is based on the belief that there are a variety of intellectual competencies. The eight areas of intelligence he recounts include

1. Linguistic—the ability to use and appreciate language and to analyze, teach, convince, and entertain
2. Spatial—the ability to conjure up and then transform mental imagery and to produce a graphic likeness of spatial information
3. Kinesthetic—the ability to control physical motion and handle objects skillfully
4. Logical-mathematical—the ability to use complex reasoning and think abstractly, with a sense of order sequence, cause and effect, and problem-solution
5. Musical—the ability to use musical elements such as pitch, rhythm, and timbre and a proclivity toward musical composition and performance
6. Interpersonal—the ability to detect and discriminate moods, intentions, and desires of others
7. Intrapersonal—the ability to know oneself and one's feelings, moods, and desires
8. Naturalist—the ability to understand, categorize, classify, and explain the natural world

Gardner further states that teachers can use these different areas of intelligence as a methodology for teaching a variety of subjects. Because children have a variety of intellectual strengths and passions, we decided our reading comprehension project needed to be based on a broad definition of intelligence. Therefore, we thought children would acquire the comprehension strategies more readily when we incorporated the arts because the arts involve multiple intelligences.

Multiple Sign Systems

Often, teachers use drama, drawing, block building, or clay sculpting as avenues for students to share their thinking about reading. As we reflected on children's use of the arts, we became aware of ways they were using both the arts and language to understand new concepts. This is expressed best by the theory of multiple sign systems. The theory is based on the idea that each art form uses its own unique set of symbols and signs to express meaning. Furthermore, people's semiotic system, or process of making meaning in a culture, is based on their ability to weave together sign systems to make meaning. For example, in *Picture This: How Pictures Work*, Molly Bang (2000) explores how line, shape, color, and composition in a picture are interpreted by the viewer. In one picture, for example, she illustrates this point by drawing a tilted tree. By seeing the tree in this position and seeing the implied motion, the viewer thinks the tree is going to fall. This interpretation is based on the viewer's cultural and personal awareness about how artists depict motion in artwork.

Learning about multiple sign systems illuminated for us that the arts could not only engage students in learning, but also help them gain meaning. As students gain meaning through multiple sign systems, they bring together various strands of understanding to develop complex meaning from text. Marie Emmitt (1998) points out the significance of developing multiple sign systems: "Ideally, we should be conversant with a range of ways of making meaning and have the choice to select whatever mode is most appropriate for our purposes. In many contexts we need to use a number of ways" (p. 2). Integrating the arts in the teaching of reading comprehension strategies allows students to develop a rich source of sign systems that merge a deep understanding of the arts, the comprehension strategies, and text.

Cognitive Development and the Multisensory Approach

Our research on the arts and cognitive development led us to the book *Smart Schools: Better Thinking and Learning for Every Child* (Perkins, 1995), in which the author describes his views on learning. One major component of the book is the idea that in order for students to have understanding of a concept, they need to be able to actively apply their knowledge. Perkins states that mental imagery is a strong tool for helping readers gain understanding and that readers build imagery through actions. We saw Perkins's ideas in action when we used a series of tableaux to help develop the meaning of a story. To create a tableau, students use their bodies to produce a frozen scene of gestures or images that focus on an idea or event from the text. After using tableaux, students told us, "I didn't understand the story, but when I became the character, then I knew what it was about." It became apparent to us that this mental imagery was an essential element of children's reenactment of stories and of their reading comprehension.

As we used the arts to teach the reading comprehension strategies, we were surprised that children clearly articulated how the mental imagery helped them gain new meaning from text. We saw how thoroughly the arts engaged children by involving all their senses. This kind of multisensory approach invited children to be involved with what they were reading through gestures of characters, sounds of settings, and images of scenes. David Perkins describes this multisensory approach in *The Intelligent Eye: Learning to Think by Looking at Art* (1994). He specifically discusses the following features of art that build strategic thinking:

- Sensory anchoring: having a physical object to focus on as you think and talk and learn
- Instant access: the immediacy of an artwork or dramatic presentation
- Personal engagement: works of art are made to draw and hold attention
- Dispositional atmosphere: broad and adventurous thinking
- Wide-spectrum cognition: inclusive, multisensory style of thinking
- Multiconnectedness: art allows for rich connection making (pp. 83–85)

By highlighting these natural qualities inherent when working with the arts, we were able to help students develop expertise in learning and using the comprehension strategies.

Final Thoughts

When we first taught reading comprehension strategies using the arts, we observed students giving thoughtful responses and wondered how and if they would be able to transfer their understanding of these strategies to their reading of text. We learned that this transference across disciplines was difficult for our students. However, as John Bransford, Ann Brown, and Rodney Cocking state in *How People Learn: Brain, Mind, Experience, and School* (2000),

> Knowledge that is taught in only a single context is less likely to support flexible transfer than knowledge that is taught in multiple contexts. With multiple contexts, students are more likely to abstract the relevant features of concepts and develop a more flexible representation of knowledge. (p. 78)

By teaching a strategy such as questioning through multiple contexts such as paintings, music, poetry, and movement, we thought students would develop multidimensional understandings of the strategy. This, in turn, would help make the transference to text easier.

What also became apparent to us as we taught these strategies was that in order for students to transfer their understanding of a comprehension strategy, we—as teachers—played a significant role by scaffolding the ideas generated from the class in order to maintain the momentum and focus of the work. We used the following three major strands of scaffolding to help students build bridges to text: thoughtful preparation, high-level questioning, and authentic participation in the arts lessons.

Deliberately organizing the purpose and goals of the project was the backbone of our preparation. One aspect of our planning was critically choosing text and arts lessons that would build on one another to develop a higher level of comprehension. We always chose text and art in order to offer students easy entry into learning new concepts.

We also consistently helped students clarify and reflect on their thinking through the questions we asked. We invited students' creative thinking through the brainstorming process and modeled strategic questioning to show them how to focus on noteworthy ideas. Through our questioning, we also gently helped students filter out extraneous details and highlight significant insights. The use of webs, charts, drawings, and photographs helped students see the connections in their questioning and retain important concepts.

Finally, we scaffolded work for the students by participating in the arts lessons. As we joined in on tableaux, became characters in dramatic interviews, or sent letters in a process drama, we were able to set expectations, stretch students' thinking, and clarify confusion. This participation also showed students that we valued learning through the arts.

The following chapters show the role we played in the students' learning, but more important, these chapters demonstrate how students successfully transferred their learning.

Chapter 2

Developing Sensory Images

It is impossible even to think without a mental picture.

—Aristotle, trans. 1972, p. 14

On a hot late spring afternoon, three girls stand outside Sabine's second-grade classroom door to greet parents and visitors who have come for our Amazon celebration. On the door, the students have posted a quiz for daring adventurers (see Figure 1). The girls start to read aloud the questions to the assembled group of parents and visitors and wait for their replies.

Then, the girls open the door and let the crowd enter the Amazon: A blue paper river snakes its way across the floor; a canoe sits in the middle of the river; plants cover the desks; humidifiers blow steam into the air; and sounds of the rain forest, such as birds squawking and rain falling, fill the room. Students guide the parents and visitors around the edge of the class. The visitors marvel at the students' work, which includes wire-sculpture jaguars and toucans, a 20-foot-long papier-mâché anaconda, shaman masks, clay insect tiles, a collage-mural of the various layers of the rain forest, and written

Figure 1   Amazon Quiz

Before going to the Amazon you should answer these questions.

How would you like have sweat flies all over you?
Are you afraid of 30 ft. snakes?
Would you be sick if you had to eat termites?
What would you do if a wart hog were chasing you?
Can you imagine going for weeks in the hot humid rainforest with out a shower?
Your ready. Well if your not ready for all of this then you better not go!

reports on various animals. The celebration ends with two theatrical performances based on folk tales from the Amazon, *The Dancing Turtle: A Folktale From Brazil* (DeSpain, 1998) and *Papagayo, the Mischief Maker* (McDermott, 1980).

The seed for this idea of turning the class into a rain forest grew from the original performance of these plays in class and the students' desire to re-create the Amazon. They wanted their parents to know what it would be like to spend time in the rain forest. The students wanted it to look like a jungle, but they also wanted everyone to *feel* the heat and humidity in the air and *hear* the overwhelming drone of insects and birds. The children supplied us with detailed descriptions of what to include and how to design the perfect atmosphere.

The students' dedication to details and images showed us that they had developed deep imagery of the Amazon region from the books and projects of our in-class study. In his book *Cognition and Curriculum Reconsidered*, Elliot Eisner (1994) states, "One must be able to experience something in order to know it" (p. 29). The students knew that in order for their parents to understand all they had learned, the parents needed to experience the Amazon.

Developing powerful imagery is significant in a reader's ability to comprehend text. Teachers know that making mental constructs and creating imagery help readers organize information, develop memory, and assimilate details to help create a holistic understanding. We found that through the use of the arts, students developed a strong understanding of the concept of imagery, which they then were able to use in their reading. We discovered that at times, an artistic process deepened students' imagery about a particular text and helped develop comprehension of that text. The arts also were a means for reaching a broader range of students. For a few students who often had been unable to communicate their understanding of texts, the arts finally enabled them to express their thoughts.

What Is Developing Sensory Images?

Sensory imagery occurs when readers use all their senses (smell, taste, touch, sound, and visualization), their emotional responses to a piece of writing, and their prior knowledge about the topic to create complex, multidimensional scenes that help them gain lasting meaning from the story. While reading and thinking about imagery, we realized that there were many differing ideas about its meaning. Exploring further, we concluded that one important part of imagery is the mental construct a person develops, often from prior knowledge, in order to help gain meaning. For example, if a person says he or she is taking a trip to Europe, the statement evokes a specific mental response in others. For one person, this statement conjures thoughts of the smell of fresh bread, the image of crowded trams, the feel of cobblestone streets, and the sound of a grandmother's laugh. For another person, this same statement brings to mind a famous museum, war in the Balkans, and a family strudel recipe. Even though their thoughts are different, both individuals have a multidimensional mental construct of Europe that provides them the basis from which they can interpret new information. This type of mental construct involves visualization but often includes much more, such as the use of prior knowledge and input from the other senses.

Visualization is often equated with sensory imagery, and although this is an important aspect of imagery development, it does not stand alone. Imagine making popcorn. The first thing many people think about is the sound of the kernels popping or the smell of the popcorn. This type of imagery goes beyond visualization. Sensory imagery relies on all the senses, encompassing mental impressions of smells, tastes, movements, and sounds. While reading, these images allow readers to create holistic mental images. This type of imagery often leads people who have read a book to feel disappointed when they see the movie version of the book. Research by Shirley Long, Peter Winograd, and Connie Bridge (1989) concluded that developing a sensory image helps a reader increase working memory by allowing him or \her to incorporate details. It also supports the reader in making analogies and comparisons. For instance, when reading a book about medieval castles, a student who has visited a castle might compare the size of the castle in the book to a castle he or she has visited. Imagery also offers a tool through which readers can organize and store meaning gained while reading.

In her book *Visualizing and Verbalizing: For Language Comprehension and Thinking* (1991), Nanci Bell points out that throughout history, developing imagery has played various roles. In Ancient Greece, teachers explicitly taught students how to create an image to help memorize and comprehend text and stories. However, in recent times, there has been an underlying assumption that all students inherently cultivate imagery, and few teachers explicitly teach students how to visualize. Bell indicates that many students still need to be taught how to create images from texts. Further, her book focuses on teaching students how to determine what words in the text develop images.

Using the Arts to Teach Sensory Imagery

Even at a basic level, the arts encourage the creation of imagery. Whether dancing across a stage, painting a blank canvas, or playing a piece of music, the artist comes to the endeavor with some sensory image. This natural aspect of the arts can help build students' understanding and use of sensory imagery to express meaning. By engaging students in artistic expression, you can use the arts to support reading comprehension because the arts allow students to develop imagery that assimilates more complex concepts and details about the text. This facilitates students' abilities to build rich mental constructs about the text. Perhaps the most noticeable aspect of using the arts in the development of sensory images is that the arts are inherently multisensory: The arts expose students to communicating their ideas through movement, pictures, sounds, and gestures. The arts approach builds a more complex understanding of sensory imagery, and the multisensory dimension of the arts enables a broad range of students to learn this strategy.

The second-grade students' Amazon rain forest celebration, described in depth in the following section, was a tribute to all they had learned. The celebration helped them organize and understand the details and significant concepts learned in our rain forest study and use that information in a meaningful way.

An In-Depth Look at Teaching Imagery Through a Study of the Amazon Rain Forest

When we started our journey using the arts to teach reading comprehension strategies, teaching students about the significance of sensory images while reading seemed to hold a natural connection to many artistic endeavors. We chose to focus on this strategy while studying the Amazon rain forest, a region full of powerful images. Choosing to focus on sensory images during a study of the Amazon also allowed us to encourage students to use this strategy while reading nonfiction text. During our exploration of developing sensory imagery, we engaged in the artistic mediums of improvisational drama and drawing.

Using Improvisational Drama and the Sensory Wheel to Introduce Imagery

The second graders sat on the floor in front of the rocking chair where Sabine was sitting. They realized that something was amiss because they could not see the title or front cover of the book that was being read, *Journey Through a Tropical Jungle* (Forsyth, 1988):

> With no wind and no shade, sweat was pouring off my forehead. The droplets made muddy streaks in the road dust coating my face. It was just too hot to be out in the sun. My only companions were the tiny doves that flushed up from the roadside and then settled in the grasses. (p. 11)

Sabine stopped the reading at this point in the text and asked the students to use their bodies, not their words, to show how it would feel to be there. Students draped their bodies around the floor and were hanging off one another. Some wiped their brows, and others fanned themselves. After a minute, we asked them, "What does it sound like there?" Some students sat silently, but others started making sizzling and buzzing sounds. Then, we asked the students to describe what a picture would look like if they painted this scene. "I'd have lots of insects flying," Sara responded. Jason added, "I'd draw sweat dripping off my face." We next had students discuss which part of the passage evoked the strongest image for them. On the chalkboard, we kept a list of the words or phrases the students shared, such as *hot, loud, sweaty, tired,* and *green.* After compiling this list, Sabine continued reading but stopped periodically to ask the students more questions about how it might look, smell, sound, taste, or feel in the rain forest. The students were thrilled to be able to hoot like howler monkeys or hold their noses when they listened to the description of the smell of rotting fruits and flowers. They each found some way of expressing meaning through their actions. This improvisational drama helped build the students' multisensory imagery about the rain forest, as they quickly moved beyond the pictures in the book to images of the smell, sound, and feel of the rain forest.

The next time we met, we passed out sensory wheels to the students. Sensory wheels are circular pieces of paper divided like a pie into five sections. The edge of each section is labeled by one of the five senses, respectively—feelings, sounds, smells, tastes, and sights.

After handing out the sensory wheels, Sabine read passages from different texts about the Amazon and asked the students to touch the section of the wheel that indicated which image was the strongest in their mind. For example, was it the feel of rain on their skin or the crunch of an insect for dinner? After listening to the first passage, students turned their wheels to a sense and shared what they thought were the most powerful images from that passage. One student, Calvin, raised his hand and asked, "What happens if I had a strong feeling about what it would taste like and also how it smelled?" Although most students started by sharing just one image, we welcomed all students' thoughts. As Sabine read other passages, more students began to share multiple layers of imagery. During the last passage, students wrote down their imagery on the wheel (see Figure 2 for an example of one student's sensory wheel).

Figure 2   Example of Filled-In Sensory Wheel

As they listened to most passages, a noticeable pattern emerged: The students tended to focus on the most descriptive attribute of the text, whether visual or auditory. We also observed that regardless of the text we read, two or three students always had the same type of imagery develop. One girl, for example, always imagined the sounds first. Although she told us that she might develop other imagery later, she always "heard" things first. The class discussion after this activity focused on the fact that even though people respond differently to text, they all develop images when they read. Students realized that some people may never have any images of smells but always can imagine sounds. We then thought that perhaps the ability to develop images is linked to each student's intrinsic learning strengths.

Both the use of improvisational drama and the sensory wheel helped students become aware of the types of mental images that may surface during reading. These activities also required the students to tap into their background knowledge about heat or the sounds that insects make. The children had developed this knowledge by hearing, tasting, and touching the world around them. The drama and the sensory wheel allowed the students to transfer their prior knowledge and warehouse of images to the text we were reading to nourish their comprehension.

Using Drawing as a Pathway to Imagery

During class discussions about imagery, several students remained quiet; therefore, we introduced an activity that would depend less on students' abilities to verbalize their thinking. Because drawing seemed like the perfect way to glimpse into students' visual images of the text, we asked students to create drawings from a piece of text and then compare their drawings with those of other students. Our goal was for these comparisons to stretch students' thinking about texts and help them assimilate new images into their mental constructs.

The students had read and listened to a great deal about the Amazon rain forest by the time we introduced this lesson. Therefore, they could draw from a large pool of background information. It was difficult for us, however, to find reading material that would challenge them on the comprehension level, yet be easy enough for them to read. As we searched through books about the Amazon, we found the following passage by Sir Walter Raleigh (as cited in Gheerbrant, 1988/1992), one of the first Europeans to visit that region:

> I never saw a more beautiful country, nor more likely prospects, hills so raised here and there over the valleys, the river winding into diverse

branches, the plains adjoining without bush or stubble, all fair green grass, the ground hard sand easy to march on, either for horse or foot, the deer crossing in every path, the birds towards the evening singing on every tree with a thousand several tunes, cranes and herons of white, crimson and carnation perching on the river side. The air fresh with a gentle easterly wind, and every stone we stooped to take up, promised either gold or silver by its complexion. (pp. 45–46)

To begin our lesson, Sabine wrote Raleigh's passage on the chalkboard and gave each student a personal copy. We then shared background information about Raleigh, his expedition to the Amazon, and his attempts to convey his impression of that region to the people in England. We requested that students become the expedition's artists. In other words, it was their job to use pictures to bring to life Raleigh's words in the passage. After sharing these expectations with the students, Sabine read aloud Raleigh's passage.

During reading, we stopped to discuss why Raleigh's language and phrases sounded different. Calvin quickly informed the class that it was because the writing was from the "old times." We then asked the students to use colored pencils to underline parts that they thought painted a mental picture. Some students underlined many different words, others underlined only a few words such as *mountain* and *gold*, and a few highlighted whole phrases. Next, we passed out pastels and paper and reminded the students to create pictures that would depict the meaning of the writing. The students' pictures often included what they had underlined, but many students added more detail, creating images of the whole passage.

Observing the students as they worked made it obvious that some words in Raleigh's passage conjured up images more readily than others. For example, all the students included hills, mountains, and greenery in their drawings. But aside from these shared images, the pictures were very different. One student drew a series of small pictures, with each one highlighting a different part of the passage. Another student filled the page with colors for the bird and used gold specks to show the tan beach and footprints to represent the humans. And another student chose to create a pen-and-ink drawing rather than use the pastels we had distributed (see Figure 3).

Once the students finished their drawings, we passed them around so each person had a chance to see these creations. This was a powerful experience for the students because it demonstrated how different responses to text could be. Indeed, they showed surprise at one another's images, often impressed but also at odds over other students' depictions. Roberta then reread

Figure 3   Student's Drawing of the Amazon

the passage one last time. Students stopped the reading with comments such as "Now I get what all the animals are doing," or "I know *complexion* means *color.*" It was clear that the students felt more comfortable and confident about verbally interacting with the text after drawing their pictures. Drawing gave them the opportunity to organize their thinking about the piece. We also noticed that when creating their drawings, some students reread Raleigh's passage numerous times to gain significant details. The overall effect of this activity was that it aided the students in their comprehension of the passage.

As part of the culmination of our Amazon study, we placed four pieces of descriptive writing around the room. We thought that the students had a strong understanding of sensory imagery and were ready to transfer their learning by using the strategy without the aid of an art form. The students divided into four groups, and each group read one piece of writing and read and took notes about any images that surfaced. After 10 minutes, the groups rotated, giving everyone a chance to read each piece of writing.

As we walked around the room, we noticed some students would read, then jot down their thoughts. For many students, this was easy, as they were able to delve into the text and develop images and understanding. For example, in response to a descriptive passage about traveling by boat on the Amazon River, Allison wrote, "We are in a boat and the water is splashing the boat. I feel scared but happy. I see tall trees and green, green plants. The river is very full. There are big beautiful flowers. The day is hot on the muddy river." Another student, Clay, wrote about the importance of body painting to the indigenous people of the Amazon region: "They decorate themselves because they believe if they decorate themselves like the jungle they will have the power of the jungle." However, just as many students wrote only a few words or none at all. The text was challenging, and some students clearly had difficulty grasping meaning or even conveying any images. Many students made comments by relying solely on their background knowledge about the topic rather than an image developed in the piece of writing. For example, in response to a poem about the majesty of trees, many students wrote, "Trees give you oxygen," or "Don't cut down trees."

We decided to shift gears to help more students transfer their learning. Gathering the students together, we asked them to talk about their understanding of each piece of writing. Many children voiced frustration at not understanding what they were reading. We suggested that the students pick the one piece of writing that intrigued them and draw a picture of the images. All the students thought this was possible, and their frustration rapidly decreased.

When the students completed the pictures, we asked them to share their drawings with the class and to explain what was in the pictures and why they put it there. The difference in the students' responses was amazing. For the students who were not able to make a written response, drawing pictures brought out details that allowed them to discuss their understanding of the writing in a complex manner. For an example, see Figure 4, which shows Ella's drawing based on the following piece of writing:

> We glided slowly upstream along the banks, Bolivia on the right and Brazil on
> the left. Tall dark green trees and thick bushes sloped down to the surface of
> the water. The air was heavy as if after a rain, and the forest had the sharp odor
> of rotting earth and tropical flowers. Cicadas whined throughout the long, hot
> muggy day. The sun was a hazy yellow ball high in the sky. (Lourie, 1991, p. 8)

When Ella responded to this passage in writing, she wrote, "The jungle is wet." But her picture was full of images. As Ella discussed her drawing, she

Figure 4   Ella's Drawing That Depicts Traveling the Amazon by Boat

explained how she made the background green and added colorful flowers because the author talked about that in the text. She said that she drew "life" in the river because if people were traveling by boat, they would be able to see the things in the river. Ella also added that it would be very hot in the Amazon. Even though Ella developed imagery while she was reading, the artwork first allowed her to recall the imagery and then helped her to express her thinking with language.

We realized that perhaps we had asked some children to transfer their learning too soon. Research has shown that students have to be competent in using a skill in one area before they are able to transfer their learning to another area (Bransford et al., 2000). By working with these students and allowing them to use drawing as a reading comprehension tool, we purposely slowed down to allow all the students to use their mental construct of the Amazon to help them develop images of the passage. We also realized that some students may need to rely on drawing as a tool when they encounter difficult text. Drawing may be what allows them to visualize the text.

Developing sensory images allows readers to retain what they have read and gives them the necessary information from which new thinking about a piece of writing can develop. Often, teachers think that all students have the ability to visualize while they read because they are able to do this at play or in their artwork. As evidenced through our study of the Amazon, this is not an automatic ability for some students. Teaching students about sensory images and how to use them while they read is an important step to reading comprehension.

Art-Based Lessons for Developing Sensory Images

Using Clay Sculptures to Assimilate Details About Characters

Grades: 2–5

Materials: modeling clay (or paper or actual objects for sculptures)

Text Resources: *Sarah, Plain and Tall* (MacLachlan, 1985), *The Ballad of Lucy Whipple* (Cushman, 1996), *Aunt Clara Brown: Official Pioneer* (Lowery, 1999), and *Bess's Log Cabin Quilt* (Love, 1995)

Lesson: During a third-grade study of Colorado history and westward migration, students were in book groups. All the books had pioneering themes and strong main characters. When students finished their books, we gave each of them a large piece of clay and asked them to choose one of the main characters as the focus of clay sculptures. We explained to students that they could not re-create the actual character but had to use the clay to mold 10 items that the character would possess. Knowing that the first few items would be easier to create than the final ones, we placed a number on how many articles the students could sculpt in order to expand their thinking about the characters. We further explained that when they finished sculpting these items, the students needed to write why each item was pivotal to the character.

A few students started this activity by making a list of items they thought the character would own. Other students looked at the books again to help them think of items. In many of the stories, however, the main characters were poor and the text did not clearly state what they owned, so the students had to infer what the character might own. In the process of creating these sculptures, many students had to rely on information they had learned in other parts of our history study in order to create accurate images of the characters.

We observed that one student, Laura, was captivated by this project and made more than 10 items. Laura had read *The Ballad of Lucy Whipple* and thought that Lucy had been smart to start a business to save money to travel back home. Therefore, she created sculptures of all the ingredients that would be found in an apple pie and tried to sculpt an old-time flour sack. Laura also made a feather pen and an ink bottle to show the significance of Lucy's letter writing to her grandparents in Boston, Massachusetts, USA. This is just one example of a student who went beyond what was in the book to develop the character further.

Reflection: As the students presented each of the items they created, it became obvious that they had stretched their understandings of the characters and the texts. This lesson required that students move beyond the images presented in the text and develop more holistic images of the characters. These new images were based on students' prior knowledge and inferences made about the character.

Using Watercolor Painting to Develop Holistic Imagery

Grades: 1–5

Materials: heavy stock paper or watercolor paper, watercolor paints (pre-mixed wet paints or watercolor sets), sponges, brushes, jars for water

Text Resource: *The Dalai Lama: A Biography of the Tibetan Spiritual and Political Leader* (Demi, 1998)

Lesson: As part of a second-grade class study on heroes and heroines, we read *The Dalai Lama*. This book is filled with rich, beautiful watercolors of Tibet and the Dalai Lama's life. Because there were so many new concepts in this book, we decided to have students work on watercolor paintings of mountains similar to those in the book (see Appendix B for specifics on the technique of wet-on-wet watercolor painting). Because of our experience during the Amazon study, we believed that the process of creating a painting would compel the students to develop more elaborate sensory imagery from the text, thus supporting their comprehension of the story.

Before this lesson, we arranged the chairs in a semicircle, turned off the overhead lights, and put on quiet background music. When they streamed in from their physical-education class, the students quietly found places to sit. They paid close attention as Sabine demonstrated how to paint a mountain scene while Roberta read the story of the Dalai Lama. Roberta stopped at different points during the reading so Sabine could highlight aspects of watercolor painting.

After we finished reading, the students returned to their desks to start their own paintings. We asked them to be aware of the images that developed while they painted. A calm, peaceful atmosphere developed as the students began painting: They were focused and had few distractions. When students finished painting, we instructed them to write poems highlighting the images in their paintings. When everyone was finished, the students shared their paintings and poems. Figure 5 shows an example of one student's watercolor, and the following excerpts show poetry written by two students:

> In a blizzard at the top of the world
> Walking, searching, surviving
> Hoping for a life of peace.
>
> The frozen wind
> On top of the mountain
> And there sits the lonely village

Reflection: The students' poems were filled with images. These images provided not only what Tibet looked like but also the overall feeling of the story. These images gave clues to the weather, sounds, and sights of the Dalai Lama's story, as well as the story's emotions and hopes. Painting part of the story encouraged students to add detail to their images, which also made

Figure 5 Student's Watercolor Painting of Mountains

them check their comprehension of the text. The painting and poetry writing also helped them focus and create their impressions of the hardships, the struggles, and purpose of the journey discussed in the story.

Using Music to Introduce Sensory Imagery

Grades: K–2

Materials: tempera paint, paintbrushes, white construction paper

Music Resources: "The Apache Honoring Song" (Walela, 1996, side a), "The Entertainer" (Joplin, 1902, track 6), and other instrumental music

Lesson: To introduce imagery to a group of kindergartners, we decided to have them create paintings while listening to music. After they created their paintings, we asked them to look at their paintings to see the influence of the music. This activity gave us the opportunity to explore how different experiences create varying images.

Before the students came into the classroom, we made sure to have all the supplies ready. We placed four jars of tempera paint (each a different color) in the center of each table and placed the brushes next to the paper. The students entered the room and found a place to sit. We explained that they were to listen to the music for a minute before they began painting so they could paint what they thought the music would look like.

We played "The Apache Honoring Song," a slow, calm Native American piece. The students sat and quietly listened. When it was time to paint, most students began quickly, although there were a few students who sat still and clearly had difficulty thinking of what to paint. We closely observed these students to see if they would paint at all: Eventually, almost all the students started painting. After several minutes, we had everyone stop. Students who wanted to share with the class were given a few minutes to explain why they thought their painting matched the music. After this sharing, everyone put their paintings on the drying rack in the hall and returned to their seats.

We then played "The Entertainer," an up-tempo piece that created a great contrast to the previous piece. Again, the students sat and listened to the music before they began painting. This time, however, all the students painted. Many children quickly filled the page. A few children made designs, lines, or shapes using a great deal of color. One student, Adrian, decided to mix most of the paint and use the same brown color that he had used in his other painting. Once again, we gave students a few minutes to share their thoughts.

Reflection: After finishing the discussion, the students gathered their artwork. We hung the paintings created while listening to Tribal Voices on one side of the chalkboard and the other group of paintings next to them. Then, the students talked about what they noticed about the two groups of paintings—what was similar, what was different, did the music change the way they painted? Most of the students' comments were about the feelings and thoughts that the music produced. One student, Allison, stated that the first piece made her imagine sitting silently by the sea. The students realized "that's why she painted the ocean." Throughout the discussion, we pointed out to students when they were sharing feelings, sounds, smells, or tastes to help them create their visual images of the music. We explained that these types of thoughts and images are the same kinds that good readers use to comprehend a story. By using music and painting, students were able to develop a wide range of images that helped them learn in a detailed manner about the strategy of developing sensory images.

Using Famous Paintings to Demonstrate Analogies of Imagery

Grades: 1–5

Text Resource: *The Incredible Painting of Felix Clousseau* (Agee, 1988)

Artwork Resources: *La Meridienne (d'apres Millet)* (van Gogh, 1889), *Woman and Child Driving* (Cassatt, 1881), and other famous paintings with people as subjects

Lesson: Paintings and illustrations foster a great deal of imagery for students. Our goal with this lesson was to help first-grade students develop imagery that went beyond what they saw in each painting. We wanted them to use the paintings to spark their imaginations so they could make predictions, draw analogies, and develop meaning.

We also used *The Incredible Painting of Felix Clousseau*, which is about a painter whose pictures come to life. The story highlights the chaos that occurs when the paintings come alive: What would happen if the snake in a painting hanging on the living room wall came to life and joined you in the bathtub? This book toys with reality by playing with the concept of where a picture begins and where it ends.

Before we read this book to the class, we used the famous paintings for a drama game. Our thought was that by having students experience a painting coming to life, they would be able to make analogies to the images in the book, thus leading to better comprehension.

To begin, we placed the van Gogh print on the board so everyone could see it. *La Meridienne* shows a man and a woman relaxing on a haystack. Two students, Alex and Andrea, volunteered to place themselves in the same positions as the people in the picture. They lay on the ground while the other students helped them figure out the correct body positions. Once Alex and Andrea got the positions correct, they froze for a few minutes. Then we asked them to unfreeze but still pretend they were the people from the picture. We asked them, "What would happen next?" It was a few more minutes before Alex and Andrea were ready to move again. They were giggling and concerned about doing it right. When Alex finally moved again, he stood up and acted like he had just woken up; Andrea joined in quickly.

The other students then made comments and wanted their own turns as volunteers. We chose two more students, Jared and Hannah, to reenact the same painting. This time, however, we asked them to stand up and act out what happened right before the picture was painted. The children took a few minutes to talk about what they were going to do, then began acting it out. They swung their arms like they were cutting grass or plowing a field and talked about how hot, tired, and hungry they were. Finally, Jared interrupted, "Let's stop to rest and have a snack." At that point, they both lay down on the imaginary haystack.

After the class worked through the same process with a painting by Cassatt, Sabine read aloud *The Incredible Painting of Felix Clousseau*. At the end of the book, the artist is released from prison. The illustration on the last page shows the artist walking to the scene in a framed picture, and the words underneath the picture note, "and he returned to his painting" (n.p). When Sabine read these words, Jared jumped up and shouted, "Hey, I was in a painting, too." The illustration and play on words led to a discussion about what the author meant, as well as what might happen next. The drama activity that we had used prior to the book reading had awakened in the children a different type of thinking about the story.

Reflection: In the discussion that followed the reading of the book, Andrea said she thought the ending of the book was similar to what they had done with the paintings because the painter would now live in the picture. We asked the class if they thought having a chance to act out the story helped them understand the book. One student, Michael, commented, "I knew what they meant." But Elizabeth said, "I might have gotten confused with the word because I had never thought of a painting living." We then shared with the class that good readers often take images of what they know and compare them to what they are reading, just like the students had done with the dramatization.

In order to act out the paintings, the students had to interpret and predict the images that might have occurred before and after the scene. They also pointed out details in the painting to help explain their thinking. Alex, for example, explained, "See, the man has a hat over his eyes; he must be sleeping." We saw this as an opportunity to share with the class that good readers create images that often go beyond the text and add meaning to what they are reading. We thought that having the students learn how to focus on specific aspects of a painting to help expand their images was similar to how readers focus on specific aspects of a text to aid their comprehension. By using rich visual images and actively engaging their whole bodies, students were able to see how developing an image about one scene could help them understand a different scene.

Using Group Collage to Organize Imagery

Grades: 3–4

Materials: a sand tray (optional) or large piece of cardboard; scrap boxes or wooden blocks of various sizes; leaves, pine cones, pebbles, or left-over decorations; paper; scissors

Text Resource: *Seedfolks* (Fleischman, 1997)

Lesson: The third-grade class was reading the book *Seedfolks*. In this story, a young girl starts a neighborhood movement to create a garden. Each individual who joins the project tells his or her life story and has a unique method of gardening. The garden is created on a trash-filled lot, which is surrounded by enormous apartment buildings, in New York City. The efforts of each gardener eventually transform the lot into the heart of the neighborhood.

As the class read the book, three students—Manuel, Jonathan, and Halley—began working on the class's collage. We gave the class a large square sand tray (see Appendix B for specifics on constructing sand trays) and instructed the students to make tall buildings around the outside edge of the tray, leaving the center empty to represent the trash-filled lot. The students used wooden blocks of different sizes to create the apartment buildings. For two buildings, the students cut out little paper windows and taped them to the blocks. Then, they placed an assortment of pine cones, leaves, and pebbles in the center of the lot to represent small trash items. Manuel and Halley were the only students in the class who had been to New York City.

Because they had an understanding of how tall the buildings are and how it feels to walk down city streets that feel like canyons, we asked them to describe this to the other students. Halley and Manuel loved explaining city life to the class.

Next, we assigned pairs of students a certain character from the book. After reading that character's story, each pair created the piece of the garden that went with the individual. For instance, Bradley and Nicholas read about the character who is wheelchair bound and has to create his garden in a barrel high enough for him to plant his seeds. With this knowledge, Bradley and Nicholas cut the top off a small paper cup and filled it with dirt from the playground. They also made small paper flowers to grow out of the soil. Bradley and Nicholas completed this activity by clearing off the exact spot in the lot, or collage, in which their character had planted his part of the garden and placing their self-made barrel there.

As the students completed their respective sections of the garden, they saw the trash disappear spot by spot, replaced with paper flowers, pipe-cleaner vines, and stone paths. Indeed, the heart of this neighborhood emerged right before their eyes.

Reflection: *Seedfolks* is a series of vignettes that build on one another to reveal the characters and the neighborhood. Because the structure of this art lesson mirrored the structure of the text, it helped students organize their mental images of the garden and the city. The imagery created by the collage helped give students who had never spent time in a large city an understanding of the significance of the garden for the book's characters. As the students figured out ways to fit each character's garden into the collage, they began to create a mental map of the garden and were able to visualize how the gardens blended together. This kinesthetic activity not only allowed students to expand on the book's imagery, but also deepened their own imagery of the garden and their understanding of the connections between the vignettes, thus strengthening their comprehension of the whole story.

Using Shadow Puppets to Enhance Students' Use of Imagery

Grades: 3–5

Materials: overhead projector and colored transparencies; a white bedsheet; dark fabric; thick black construction paper or tagboard; dowels; coarse materials, such as small dried flowers and plants, and other objects for decoration; a clear Plexiglass dish; food coloring

Lesson: The fourth graders had just finished writing puppet plays. Their scripts were filled with dialogue that moved along the plot, as in most plays, but few of their scripts had descriptive language. As a class, the students were going to turn three of these plays into shadow-puppet shows that they would perform for their parents (see Appendix B for specifics on making puppets and shadow-puppet theaters, including techniques for creating backgrounds and special effects). Transforming the plays into puppet shows required the students to add imagery to the plays. To construct the sets and the puppets, students would need to read the text in a new light, adding layers of imagery that would enhance viewers' comprehension. Through this process, we hoped that the students' comprehension of the text would also increase.

To begin, students watched a short shadow-puppet show that Jan, the fourth-grade teacher, and two students presented. We made a simple shadow-puppet screen by using an overhead projector for the light source and hanging a white bedsheet for the screen. Dark fabric covered the bottom half of the sheet so viewers could not see the performers. The overhead projector sat on a desk behind the sheet, and the performers knelt behind the dark half of the screen and raised the puppets into the light (see Figure 6).

Figure 6   Students Participating in a Puppet Show

When the show ended, we shared with students how to make a puppet and some special effects that could be used. Then, the whole class chose the three plays they would perform and which part each student would perform. The students first decided what play they wanted to do, then broke into three groups. Each group read the script and wrote a list of what needed to be done for the three main elements of the play: (1) puppets, (2) backgrounds, and (3) sound effects.

Students from each group worked on these main elements—some designed sets and backgrounds, others created sound effects, and the remainder crafted puppets. In one corner, we had laid scissors, black construction paper, and dowels on a large table for the students to make the puppets. We also provided some decorative items such as small dried flowers and feathers that students could attach to their puppets. In another corner, we supplied blocks, sticks, and instruments to use for sound effects. Students working on sound effects spent time reading over their scripts to determine what sounds would work best at certain points throughout the play. The group of students working on the backgrounds drew scenes on transparencies and added details by cutting out objects such as a railroad tracks to place on top of the background. They also added different special effects to create the illusion of moving water or a colorful sky.

On the second day of this lesson, groups took turns practicing their puppet shows and putting together all the elements. At first, the performances were shaky, and students were concerned that a scene did not match the script and wanted to add humor into the puppets' movement without making it confusing. But the final performances went smoothly. Unlike the original scripts, these scenes were filled with sensory imagery. For example, in one scene in which the character is trying to blow up a rock, the narrator's words matched the movement of the characters, which coincided with a loud explosion and burst of color in the background.

Reflection: Throughout this lesson, the students puzzled over how to integrate the various imagery. As the students created each scene of the puppet show, they thought about new sound and light effects and puppetry movements that would enliven the scene. As a result, students had to reread the plays and create new images. One outcome of this lesson that we had not anticipated was that students noticed weaknesses in their plays. One girl was surprised that one group had not included more talking in a scene, and another student said he thought there should have been more details about what the "miner's trading store looked like." After comments such as these, the class decided to add these missing details to the script. The process of creating a puppet show helped students develop multisensory mental constructs of the plays, which increased their awareness of the role imagery plays in reading.

Final Thoughts

This chapter showed how students used drama, drawing, music, clay sculpting, and painting as pathways to create sensory images about what they were reading. By engaging with text through multiple sign systems, students were able to assimilate these images and create more complex meaning. The arts provided a way for students to comprehend text and learn about the comprehension strategy of developing sensory imagery.

Chapter 3

Building and Activating Schema

When children create, they are
making sense of the world.

—Roger Alexander (as cited in Cornett, 1998, p. 38)

Micaela is an 11-year-old who is a talented young dancer: She has danced since she was 4 years old. When she struggles with her research project one day, we suggest she use dance to help her understand the ideas the author presents in his book about migration. Micaela learned to read early in kindergarten but gradually fell behind because she struggles with comprehension. She can relate to pieces of information but has difficulty with the whole story.

Because she is a kinesthetic learner, we think dance will help her build schema for the text and support her in understanding the whole idea. We suggest that Micaela take sections of a book and create minidances to portray the ideas or emotions within each section. Micaela is so excited and tells us, "I go to sleep at night thinking of choreography for dances."

One weekend, Micaela works on her dance. When she returns to school and shares her dance, we know she has captured the essence of the whole text. Her dance is beautiful, and her sharing of the text is thoughtful. She wisely uses space to show how long and hard the journey in the book is, rhythm and bursts of energy to show emotions of the people migrating, and strong gestures to indicate significant moments from the text. Everything about dance awakens a kinesthetic intelligence in Micaela that helps her make meaning of the text.

For her research project during our study of migration and immigration, Micaela chose to use *The Great Migration: An American Story* (Lawrence, 1993). Jacob Lawrence's book tells of African Americans' migration from the southern United States to the urban cities of the northern states during World War I. Lawrence's narrative is compelling, as are the paintings that depict people on a journey walking, working, and traveling. For Micaela, dance seemed like an appropriate response to these paintings and narrative, which both focus on movement. Once Micaela completed her dance, we planned to help her take the pieces and create a whole. Bell (1991) states that

Reading comprehension requires automatic imaging in which parts are visualized and automatically brought together in the form of more images in order to develop a whole (gestalt) of information read. Individuals without this ability will have a reading comprehension dysfunction that cannot be corrected by just reading more material and answering questions. (p. 20)

Ultimately, dance gave Micaela the schema she needed to understand the text: She was able to build personal, emotional, and kinesthetic connections to the story. More important, however, is the fact that Micaela felt she had an opportunity to work in her primary learning mode, and dancing about the text of the book apparently made her feel confident, exuberant, and smart.

The ability to build and activate schema through a sensory experience such as dance creates tools for students to think critically about what they are reading. The connections made are memorable because they are the students' own connections. When students are given opportunities to generate connections in their own way, the creative problem solving adds to their confidence in building meaning.

What Is Building and Activating Schema?

Building schema is the process of making connections. Making connections appears simple at first, but this process is complex because these connections involve cognitive, emotional, and cultural elements that contribute to readers' understanding of the text. Also, each individual's background knowledge is unique and brings a different flavor to the text.

When reading, people make different kinds of connections. Teachers model or label the connections students make so children are able to distinguish between text-to-self, text-to-text, and text-to-world connections. Children frequently make text-to-self connections when sharing a personal story they are reminded of when reading. Sometimes, they make a text-to-text connection by comparing a text they are reading with another book they have read. Eventually, however, students will make text-to-world connections when books remind them of events, issues, or places from around the world. Being aware of these connections allows students to build understanding of the text by relating it to what they already know, thereby providing a mental model to scaffold new ideas. These rich connections also help build long-term memory about the story or information from the story.

Using the Arts to Build and Activate Schema

An integrated arts program uses artwork and music to help build and activate schema before reading text. We found that the arts can reach children at many levels of intelligence. Some students were able to respond quickly to art or music with an intellectual or emotional connection when making connections to text was still too difficult for them. Students who struggled with reading and reading comprehension were able to learn the strategies and build confidence before they confronted the text. And other students were able to use this alternative arts approach to build schema for the text. School curricula should take diverse learning styles into account by "expanding the channels through which students have the opportunity to learn; not all students need to pass through the eye of a written text" (Eisner, 1994, p. 65).

We have recorded the many ways our students responded personally to art or text. These responses might include text-to-self, text-to-text, or text-to-world connections. Students made connections to an experience, a memory, a dream, an idea, or an image from their imaginations. Or, they often remembered a character from another book, another piece of art, or another scene from a play or movie. All these connections worked together to build a rich schema for understanding art and text.

We used the arts to support the implementation of the reading comprehension strategy of building and activating schema by modeling what the strategy is and how it is used. At times, we used paintings as a model. For example, children studied a colorful painting of sunflowers and made connections to a grandmother's garden or a trip to a farmer's market on a Saturday morning. By making connections to visual images in art, children recognized that they could use this reading comprehension strategy quite naturally. That is, when children used their strongest intelligence to learn a new strategy, it was easier for them to transfer the use of that strategy to their reading of text. When listening to music, children made connections to a party at their house or a time when their mother played the piano. Music also evoked strong connections for children, because it helped them to understand the strategy better.

Other times, we used the arts to help students build schema before reading a particular text. That is, the arts enabled us to teach students to use their prior knowledge to understand what they were reading. Sometimes, a text or art piece was so new to the children or the text had such an unfamiliar structure that the children needed to understand before they read, so we needed to spend time building schema by giving children specific experiences or helpful information. The following section illustrates how one teacher, Jan, used the arts activity of creating sock dolls to build students' prior knowledge before reading.

An In-Depth Look at Teaching Schema Through the Art of Sock Dolls

Jan, mentioned previously, is also a third-grade teacher at our school. She regularly integrates the arts and literacy learning in her classroom and sees the literary arts as a grand interaction between the heart of an author and the heart of a child. Whenever Jan introduces a text, she believes she must prepare the children for the text as a gardener would prepare the soil for a new garden. Having just put in three new gardens on our school grounds, we understand that this process involves some strenuous digging, additional amendments to the Colorado clay soil, and patience as we watch the small plants take root. For Jan, preparing her students for a new text means opening their hearts and minds to new ideas. And that means planning her daily schedule to give children's ideas room to grow. Therefore, she starts the day with an intriguing open-ended art project and later savors the text with the children.

Jan invited us to observe her class as she used the arts to prepare students for a piece of literature, so we could work together to build students' connections to reading comprehension. The book Jan chose as the centerpiece of her introduction to Native American studies and Colorado history was Tomie dePaola's *The Legend of the Bluebonnet: An Old Tale of Texas* (1983). In this book, a young Native American girl sacrifices her doll as a way to bring rain to her land, thus saving her people. In order to help the children make connections to this girl and better understand the meaning of her sacrifice, Jan invited everyone to bring in their old socks to make sock dolls (for specifics on the technique of creating sock dolls, see Appendix B). Each child watched as Jan modeled how to create a sock doll. She had scavenged garage sales and had a substantial collection of materials for embellishing dolls' hair and clothes. The children had beads; feathers; buttons; leather, wool, and other fabric scraps; wigs; and much more to choose from as they fashioned their own sock dolls (for an example, see Figure 7).

Once they completed their dolls, Jan had the students spend time developing a connection with them. During this time, students named their dolls, wrote about special qualities their dolls possessed, and brought their dolls home one weekend to record a day in the life of their dolls. When the children had developed a visible affinity to their dolls, Jan decided to read

Figure 7　Student's Sock Doll

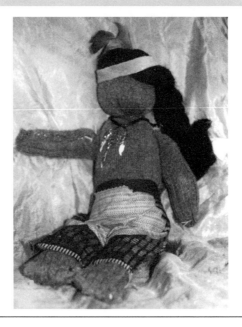

aloud *The Legend of the Bluebonnet.* As the story unfolded, the students were able to see that the girl was thinking about sacrificing her doll and were gripped by her problem, or conflict. Some students begged that she not give up her doll, and one student remarked, "I could never give up my doll."

When Jan finished reading the story, she asked the students to make connections between their experience with their dolls and the girl in the story and her doll. Jan believed that an intense experience in the arts related to a powerful text would stay in a child's memory and create new learning pathways. The conversations that followed showed the students' depth of understanding and the respect they had for the girl's incredible sacrifice. The children responded to the text by sharing memories of their own sentimental childhood objects and making connections to times in which they had given up a special toy or blanket. The impact of this shared experience was illustrated by the following student journal entry about the book:

> Legend of Bluebonnet
> There isn't going to be any doll sacrifice here!

Jan observed that the three-dimensional nature of doll making helped students who struggled with meaning because it allowed them to build schema for the story in a very concrete, visual way. The dolls allowed them to develop relationships with artwork they could hold and bring places. Having built prior knowledge through doll making, students were then able to find the words for reflection and discussion. We also noticed that the writing they did after they made their dolls showed many more connections to the text than they would have been capable of making before they created pieces of art.

After they heard *The Legend of the Bluebonnet,* we encouraged students to make connections as they read independently or participated in our book club. We asked them to mark the passages they felt connected to by writing a word that reminded them of their thoughts on a small yellow sticky note and placing the note on the page. They had become so proficient at using this reading comprehension strategy that they always had a few connections to share from the book they were reading. More important, however, was that students also started using this strategy in many areas of school. When teachers read aloud books, students would raise their hands and say, "I have a connection." Or, students would make connections during science experiments or when other students were sharing. These students' comments made it clear that this strategy benefited their understanding of books read independently or listened to as part of a class read-aloud.

Because so much of children's abilities to understand a book depends on their prior knowledge, finding ways to help them access that knowledge while reading is imperative. Our goal was to use the arts to highlight how people make connections. We believed that once students understood that they could make connections in the arts, they would transfer that understanding to text. Research shows that when a new concept or strategy is taught in a variety of ways and learners discover that the strategy can be applied extensively, then learners can use the concept or strategy more fluently (Gick & Holyoak, as cited in Bransford et al., 2000). We were encouraged to see that bringing this strategy to the forefront of the students' minds had given them a powerful method of interacting with books and their world.

Art-Based Lessons for Building and Activating Schema

Using an Artist Study of van Gogh to Build Schema

Grades: 1–5

Materials: pencils, colored chalk, tempera paints, paintbrushes, tagboard

Text Resources: *Painting the Wind: A Story of Vincent van Gogh* (Dionetti, 1996) and *The First Starry Night* (Isom, 1997)

Music Resource: "Vincent" (McLean, 1980, track 3)

Art Resource: any van Gogh painting(s)

Lesson: Everyone who passed the third-grade classroom paused at the doorway and smiled. On this particular Monday morning, the students were dancing to "Vincent," Don McLean's tribute song to van Gogh. Our special education teacher and resident flamenco dancer, Sara, was holding hands with one student, Tessa, and dancing. Tessa looked captivated.

The class was in the midst of a study of van Gogh's paintings. Their teacher, Jan, had asked us to suggest a challenging text that she could use to teach her students how to build schema. We told Jan she might find this type of higher-level text in the letter correspondence between van Gogh and his brother Theo.

Because of Jan's beliefs about the importance of building prior knowledge, the children studied van Gogh's paintings before Jan exposed them to any text. The children also learned new painting techniques (see Appendix B for specifics on using Impressionist tempera painting for a van Gogh study). Jan let the students take their paints outside just as van Gogh did. The children experienced the wind blowing their papers, allowing them to connect to van Gogh's complaint about that in his letter to his brother. Then, early one starry evening, students and their parents met Jan to paint by candlelight. After painting, they read picture books that presented stories of van Gogh in narrative form—*Painting the Wind* and *The First Starry Night*—further helping students get to know van Gogh. Next, Jan chose excerpts from Vincent's letters to his brother for the class to read and then reflect on through writing and discussion.

Reflection: The rich discussions that followed indicated that Jan's work to build an experiential understanding of van Gogh helped the children relate to the text in depth. Figure 8 is an example one third grader's written reflections on van Gogh and shows the student's level of understanding (the excerpt from van Gogh's 1888 letter to his brother is taken from letter number 472 on the Vincent van Gogh Gallery website). After an evening of painting the stars herself, this child better understood the challenges faced by van Gogh. Children encountering new and demanding text are more successful comprehending it when teachers prepare students with relevant experiences and prior knowledge. When we have introduced a new author, this reading comprehension strategy has helped us to make students more aware of the author's style and approach.

Figure 8   Third Grader's Written Reflections on van Gogh

Name **Julia**

Read this passage from Vincent Van Gogh's letter to his brother Theo and share your comments.

"If one draws a willow as if it were a living being- and after all, it really is- then the surroundings follow in due course if one has concentrated all one's attention only on that same tree, not giving up until one has put some life into it."

when You Paint You have to really get into it and You're really focused on it and You don't want to stop. You can't just draw a tree You have to express Yourself and Paint from Your heart.

Using a Study of Music and Dance to Build Schema for a Cultural Movement

Grades: 4–5

Text Resources: *Dave at Night* (Levine, 1999), *Duke Ellington: The Piano Prince and His Orchestra* (Pinkney, 1998), *Harlem: A Poem* (Myers, 1997), and *Uptown* (Collier, 2000)

Music Resource: music by Duke Ellington, such as "Mood Indigo" (1931, track 8, disc 2) and "Take the 'A' Train" (Ellington & Strayhorn, 1939, track 7, disc 1)

Lesson: The sounds of Duke Ellington rang out from our classroom, in which fifth graders in Roberta's book club were learning about jazz of the Harlem Renaissance period from 1920 to 1930. We had just finished reading *Duke Ellington: The Piano Prince and His Orchestra* and had invited our favorite piano teacher, Norma, to come help us understand more about jazz. Norma treated us to a concert of "Take the 'A' Train," as well as other Duke Ellington tunes such as "Mood Indigo."

The students needed prior knowledge of the Harlem Renaissance for the book we began reading next, *Dave at Night*. Gail Levine wrote this book based on the true story of her father, a young boy abandoned to an orphanage, who sneaks out at night and experiences the music, poetry, and creativity of the Harlem Renaissance. Without the students having a clear vision of the difference between the losses in Dave's life and the richness of the artistic life he encounters in Harlem, we thought they would not be able to comprehend how Dave uses drawing to counteract the misery at the orphanage. Therefore, we took time to teach the students about the music, dance, artwork, and poetry of this period. We wanted our students to feel as much of the magic of those times as we could re-create in our little school.

We experienced the Harlem Renaissance as we danced the Charleston, studied jazz, and read the poetry of Langston Hughes and the writings of W.E.B. Du Bois. We soaked in the words of the picture books *Harlem: A Poem* and *Uptown*. The students tried to imagine what it would be like to live in a time and place where music, dance, and art abounded and were part of everyday life.

One student who was not in our book club and, therefore, did not have the same prior knowledge, read *Dave at Night* and proclaimed, "That book's not about art and music, it's just a sad story about a kid in an orphanage." The girls in our book club, however, knew that Dave's forays into Harlem nightlife—with its joyous atmosphere of trumpet sounds, the Charleston, poetry, and painting—save his life. For example, when Dave first experiences the thrill of being good at drawing he says, "A gift! I didn't just like to draw, I didn't just have the beginnings of an eye, I had a gift!" (Levine, 1999, p. 225). One of the girls in the book club, Celine, wrote in her journal, "I feel like this when I'm in a play, and I know all my lines, and I can use a lot of expression. It makes me feel like I'm really an important part of the play." The girls in our book club knew how to reference their own past experiences of drawing strength from artistic expressions.

Reflection: Building schema for this text helped these students do the in-depth work necessary for a rich experience with the text. Understanding the cultural context helped them develop broader understanding of the author's work. This understanding provided them with the opportunity to understand the author's message in a way that changed their thinking about the text and their own lives.

Using Photographs to Make Meaningful Connections

    Grades: 2–5

    Material: disposable camera

    Text Resource: *The Journey* (Stewart, 2001)

    Lesson: Sarah Stewart's story of a young Amish girl's first trip from a farm to a big city, Chicago, was a gift to us as we taught second graders the strategy of building and activating schema. Each day of the girl's trip presents her with a wondrous new experience, and each new experience reminds her of something back home. The girl enriches her journey as she weaves these memories with new experiences.

We used photo journals to help the children develop prior knowledge and have an experience with art similar to the young girl's experience in *The Journey*. We shared with students travel journals and books of photography and highlighted how photographers choose subjects and write about their photos when they publish those types of books. Then, we asked the children to photograph something in school that was meaningful for them. Specifically, we encouraged them to make personal connections to the photos they chose to take. Each child had an opportunity to use a disposable camera to take two photographs. Once the photos were developed, we passed them back to the students so they could write a poem or short story to go with each photograph. When the students completed the writing, we hung their photos with the writings in our school gallery for display during open enrollment so visitors could see what the school meant to the children.

At the same time, Roberta read *The Journey* to the class. The students told us that their experience of taking photos was similar to the girl's experience in the story. Many students even felt that they were using their prior knowledge as they chose which photos they would take. They mainly chose photos that held special significance for them, as each photo reminded them of an important memory or image. Thus, the children easily related to both the story and the way prior knowledge worked to give more meaning to their experiences.

Reflection: During this lesson, we focused on challenging children to make meaningful connections. At first, in their eagerness to participate, students' ideas for photos were repetitive and only marginally related to the topic. To stimulate their creativity, we showed them how a photo gallery needed to include photos that were original and told a meaningful story. Gradually, this began to push the students to think more creatively. Although their display in the school gallery included the usual photos of friends, teachers, books, and projects, there was also a photo of student artwork showing the students' pride in creating a beautiful school.

Using Storytelling and Mask Making to Build Text-to-Text Connections

Grades: K–3

Materials: drums, recorder, or other musical instrument (for musical reenactment); one plastic gallon milk jug per student, newspaper, liquid starch, paint and other materials for decoration (for milk-jug masks)

Text Resources: *Peace Tales: World Folktales to Talk About* (MacDonald, 1992) and *The Drums of Noto Hanto* (James, 1999)

Lesson: Much of our community-building time in grades K–2 focused on creative problem solving. We began with storytelling because it holds students' attention, gives them an opportunity to think about important topics or values in another context, and introduces a variety of ways to solve problems. We also use stories from a variety of cultures and reenact some events in the text so children have a deeper understanding of the values in the story. Remember, however, that when teaching stories from a variety of cultures, it is vital to build authentic connections to these cultures. It is also necessary to build positive connections to replace any stereotypes that students may have. This has worked best for us by inviting people who are part of the culture we are studying to come to our classroom to share life experiences.

We like to alternate storytelling with reenactments of real-life situations that students bring to our meetings. Parents are welcome to come to school during these sessions to talk with us about how they solve problems. This opportunity allows students to transfer their knowledge from role-playing to real life. Children have learned a multitude of problem-solving responses by watching family members, friends, teachers, and other students.

When we focus on creative problem solving, one of our favorite stories to use is from Margaret Read MacDonald's book *Peace Tales*. This story, "Understanding Through the Arts or Music to Soothe the Savage Beast," is based on historical legends from Japan. It relays the story of a musician who is on his way home from a trip when pirates attack him. Even though he is sure he will die, the musician takes out his instrument and yells to the pirates that he will play them some music first. The pirates agree and listen while the musician plays soulfully. Ultimately, the pirates go away without hurting the musician because they are so taken with his music. This story brings about long discussions with students about how to use their own cleverness to solve problems. This is also a fun story to act out with children, who love to be pirates or who enjoy soothing the pirates with their recorder playing.

The next story Roberta read was similar: The storytelling provided a foundational story that we could integrate with the children's own problem-solving situations. *The Drums of Noto Hanto* tells about J. Alison James's visit to Noto Hanto, Japan, where she spoke with descendents of the original villagers who told her this story. The story reveals that original villagers used their drums (small; medium; and finally, the great *taiko*, a barrel-shaped Japanese drum) and terrifying masks (see Appendix B for specifics on making milk-jug masks) to frighten away samurai warriors who surely would have defeated them in battle. We thought this beautiful book would help build respect for using ingenious methods to solve problems. To provide the children with a similar experience to that of the villagers, we collected as many drums as we could find and set them up in a place where their noise would not intrude on other classrooms. The students then dramatized the coming of the samurai warriors and made large masks to wear while they played the drums and danced.

During a rereading of the text, we asked students to use sticky notes to mark passages that reminded them of ways *The Drums of Noto Hanto* and *Peace Tales* are alike. This experience allows children to compare similarities about characters, about the problems characters face, and about the message of each story. Also, this interpretation of the text helped them to do more than simply enjoy a story because it enabled them to find principles to use in solving their own problems.

Reflection: By the end of our storytelling and drama, we had planted the seeds for children to recall these stories when they face daily playground or classroom problems. We asked them to think like the villagers of Noto Hanto and about ways they could use the arts to solve their own problems. One young child, Michael, who struggled with whom to play at recess, simply said, "I think I will draw him a picture so he knows I want to be his friend." Also, we observed that children with linguistic strengths craved storytelling as a way of sharing, teaching, telling, and learning. These children were able to remember and use specific language from stories, and they used story naturally to make meaning.

Using Clay Work to Build Schema

Grades: 3–4

Materials: 25-pound jug of earthenware clay, decorating tools (fine-pointed tools, forks or spoons, combs, or Popsicle sticks), slip (a creamy mixture of clay and water that students can make)

Text Resources: *When Clay Sings* (Baylor, 1972), *Secrets of the Stone* (Taylor, 2000), and *A Field Guide to Rock Art Symbols of the Greater Southwest* (Patterson, 1992)

Lesson: When studying the history of the southwestern United States, we used simple clay pots and traditional decorating techniques to help third graders understand stories about the ancient art associated with this area. First, we worked with students to teach them how to make a simple coil pot from clay (for specifics on creating and decorating clay pots, see Appendix B). Then, Roberta read the book *When Clay Sings*, which describes the ancient art of decorating pots with symbols of animals, plants, and people. Another book we used, *A Field Guide to Rock Art Symbols of the Greater Southwest*, gave children inspiration for their own pot designs. We also took the students on a nature walk and asked them to observe and draw leaves, birds, flowers, and grasses. After providing these experiences, we encouraged students to use their their drawings and knowledge of design to create a design on their pots. After we fired, or dried, their pots in a kiln, children glazed or painted them, then shared their creations with the class.

After focusing on clay building and ancient designs, the children listened to a reading of *Secrets of the Stone*. Beautiful batik illustrations help Harriet Peck Taylor tell her story of a coyote and badger as they discover ancient rock art of the Southwest. These animals make their own connections to the ancient rock art. For example, the coyote's dream helps him understand the art he finds. Many of our students had traveled to see these ancient petro-glyphs and shared their connections. But even those students who had never seen actual rock art were able to make connections because they had etched similar stories on their own pots.

Reflection: Building schema for children around a historical theme helped them develop new insights about how and why certain events have occurred. By giving children an opportunity to experience an ancient artistic discipline such as designing pottery, we helped history come alive for them. Children can live out history through the arts projects you offer, and those experiences can help students build constructs for understanding themes of history.

Using Music and Dance to Teach Schema for Unfamiliar Text Structure

Grades: 1–3

Text Resource: *Hip Cat* (London, 1996)

Music Resource: any jazz or bebop music by Charlie Parker or Thelonious Monk

Lesson: Often, children encounter text with a format that is unfamiliar to them, thus hindering their comprehension. We began teaching text format to first graders by using the picture book *Hip Cat*. In this book, the words curl around the page to mirror the rhythm of the bebop and jazz music they describe. *Hip Cat* tells the story of a country cat that plays the saxophone and leaves for the city in order to find a place to earn money playing music.

Before reading the book, we played some jazz music and invited the children to demonstrate how they would move to this specific type of music. We first asked them to move along an imaginary 10- to 20-foot line. As they moved, we encouraged them to change the length and height of their movements by stretching their arms and legs. When we observed children swaying their hips, extending their arms, or creatively twisting their bodies, we acknowledged it and asked others to try the same thing until we had a combination of several pleasing movements to do together.

Afterward, we asked students to show the movements using a thin colored line on a long piece of adding machine tape. We displayed their lines and encouraged comments. The students' comments demonstrated that they understood how the music made a difference in the format of the lines. We hoped that students would then be able to simply transfer this understanding to text—that authors use different text formats to share different messages with their readers.

When Roberta read *Hip Cat* to the students, they listened quietly but moved their arms and legs with the movement of the text. They were interpreting the author's message using their bodies, and they were using prior knowledge to understand this new text format.

Reflection: We found that music and movement were effective in teaching new text structures to children. We also have used these art mediums to introduce children to the flow of poetry, as well as the variety of formats in nonfiction. When children experienced the rhythmic structure of music and used it in their movements, they formed a foundation for understanding text structure. By using an approach that relied on both musical and kinesthetic intelligences, we also reached a broader range of children, as evidenced by their engagement in learning about an important concept of text.

Final Thoughts

This chapter demonstrated how building and activating schema through the arts provided numerous connections for the children to create meaning. When children learned to rely on multiple sign systems, such as a kinesthetic approach in dance or a visual approach in painting, they gained a wide variety of resources to create meaningful connections to text. Just as fabric woven with many colors allows more interpretation than a fabric woven with one color, so does teaching with multiple sign systems. When students make a habit out of a multisensory style of thinking, they are able to access more tools to problem solve while they are reading. This rich combination of connections facilitates powerful critical thinking.

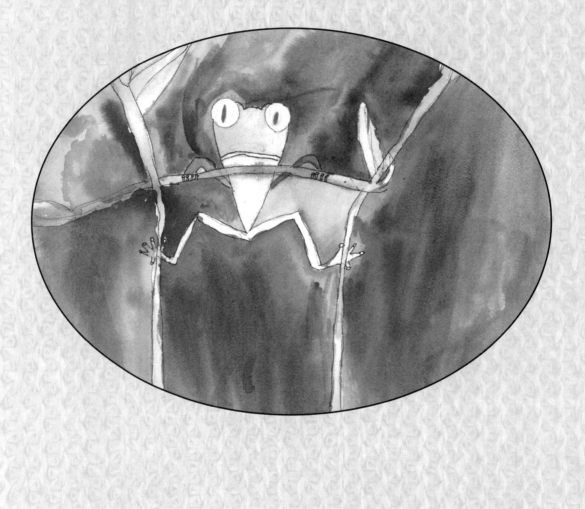

Chapter 4

Questioning

Reason can answer questions but the imagination has to ask them.

—Albert Einstein (as cited in Cornett, 1998, p. 231)

Second graders in Erin's class are reading *The Trumpet of the Swan* (White, 1970). Each day, students write in their journals and just as the character Sam Beaver does in his journal each night, end their writing with a question so they will have something to mull over while they fall asleep. They use questioning as an avenue for thinking, with journal questions such as "I practiced being quiet last night and surprising my parents. Why are cats so quiet?" and "I was playing with my sister on the weekend. Why does she ask me questions when she doesn't want to hear the answer?"

Erin is excited about the types of questions her students are asking but wants to further their learning about questioning as a reading comprehension strategy. She asks us to help expand her students' use of questioning, so we decide to take the practice of questioning further by engaging students in a dramatic interview. Using this drama technique, each student pretends to be a character in the book in order to ask other characters questions and explore ideas. In a dramatic interview with Louis, the famous trumpeting swan, the children begin by asking Hannah, who agreed to play Louis, "How did you feel when you got so much attention for playing your music?" Hannah answers, "Playing at the nightclub was too hard. There was too much talking and drinking." Then another student, Max, asks, "How was it different playing at the zoo?" Hannah responds as Louis might, "It seemed like they got a good feeling from my music. It felt like I was bringing something better into the world." Max follows up with another question, "How does music make the world better?" For an 8-year-old, Hannah answers with uncanny insight, "Music makes people stop hurrying and yelling, and then they are quiet, and they listen."

*A*t the beginning of the school year, it seemed that the children seldom asked meaningful questions about text. The few questions they did ask were intended to clarify a word or something about the plot. During dramatic interviews, however, students consistently asked important questions. Children seem to use questioning to build a coherent picture of their world. Because the arts are born from the creative place within humans, they naturally evoke curiosity and questions. By extending this natural quality of the arts, students are able to develop a deep, multidimensional understanding of questioning that helps them transfer their learning of this strategy to the comprehension of text.

What Is Questioning?

Questioning is a powerful strategy for building comprehension. As previously stated, it is the act of asking, probing, or wondering. Questioning may begin as asking for information, but it often goes beyond this to in-depth inquiry, such as pondering a controversy or discussing a problem. For young readers, the significance of this strategy lies in its ability to spark their imaginations and engage them in a piece of text. Jean Fritz describes this phenomenon in her book *Surprising Myself* (1992). She writes that there are moments while she is reading when a historic character comes alive for her. When this occurs, Fritz is driven in intense pursuit of the character. Her questions about a character take her on a journey through books, conversations, and travels. When our students engage in these kinds of questions, we know they are achieving a deep level of reading comprehension.

Many readers use questioning to self-monitor their comprehension of a text. Although this monitoring may begin with a question about vocabulary, good readers will learn to use questioning to gauge their understanding of the information presented, plot, characters, and author's intent. Indeed, questioning moves readers through a piece of writing as they pursue the unknowns of a story. For example, when a teacher finishes reading a chapter during a read-aloud of a book, students often will bombard that teacher with questions such as "What happens next?" or "Why did the character do that?" In our teaching, we have observed some children become passionate in their pursuit of a specific set of questions. Justin, for example, is a third grader who spent the first six months of the school year hounding the librarian for books about dragons. He wanted to know if dragons were real, where they lived, and what the difference was between Chinese and European dragons. Justin's desire to find answers to his questions pushed him to read further. His pursuit of dragons led him on a quest through literature.

Another style of questioning that readers may use occurs when they search for solutions pertaining to their own lives. This type of questioning is dynamic because it may lead to change and affect the way readers live or view their lives. When a friend of ours found out that he had cancer, he read everything he could find on the topic. He had focused questions about how to gain control over the various factors that lead to cancer. This pursuit for solutions changed his outlook: Instead of living in fear of his cancer, he was empowered to change his lifestyle.

Even though readers may find answers to their questions, answers are often elusive. Instead, readers may refine their questions or may be surprised by new ones. The common thread with all questioning is that it helps readers evolve their thinking.

Using the Arts to Teach Questioning

Our goal with students was to build awareness that asking questions could help them better understand stories they read. Often, the questions that students encounter in comprehension-assessment material focus only on questions with a prescribed answer. Although these questions have a significant role in students' reading comprehension, we thought it was imperative that students use questioning in a more expansive manner. Through the arts, we were able to introduce multidimensional and open-ended questioning. Research by Margaret McKeown and Isabel Beck (2001) shows that in order for students to comprehend text, questions need to leave room for students to struggle with meaning rather than just point to the answers. The very nature of the arts is such that each person's response is unique; therefore, the arts offer students the freedom to declare their own personal meaning and interpretation. This interaction with complex artistic expressions encourages students to ask sophisticated questions. When children experience questioning through various artistic mediums such as music, painting, drama, poetry, and construction, as well as text, they are able to build a rich understanding of questioning. Thus, this multidimensional mental construct provides a multitude of pathways to gain meaning from text.

The multidimensional mental construct also supports students in using questioning as a high-level comprehension strategy. We played an important role in successfully developing questioning as a comprehension strategy. We continually focused group discussion toward our purpose of building meaning. To do this, we consistently helped students clarify their thinking through the questions we asked. Another element of our job was extracting the significant ideas from thoughts students shared. We worked at scaffolding the ideas generated by the class in order to maintain the momentum and focus of the class discussion.

An In-Depth Look at Teaching Questioning Through an Artist's Work

The second-grade students had been involved in an ocean study and were reading books about oceans. We decided to start our exploration of questioning by playing music from *Pacific Blue* (Schramm, 1993), an audiotape containing instrumental music mixed with whale singing. The purpose of this activity was to engage the students in an open-ended questioning scenario. We wanted them to know that all questions were acceptable. Also, we thought that focusing the students' first questioning lesson around a piece of music rather than a book gave them a more accessible way into the process. That is, all students could participate in this exercise regardless of their reading level.

We had the students gather in a circle and explained that they were going to listen to a piece of music and try to remember any questions that came to mind as they listened. Roger asked us, "Do you mean any type of question?" Alex seemed concerned and followed with, "What happens if you don't have any questions?" We reassured the students by clarifying that even though the questions should be inspired by the music, there could be a wide range of responses. Then, each child gathered a pencil, a piece of paper, and a clipboard and settled down in a spot in which he or she felt able to concentrate.

While listening to the music, some students began to move to the beat, as others waved their pencils in the air. After a few minutes, all the children started writing. The music continued for five more minutes, and then we asked the children to join us in a circle. We gave students the opportunity to share with the class one question about the music. They produced a long list of wonderings that ranged from the technical aspects of the music to more philosophical thoughts, including the following:

- "Do whales really sing?"
- "What type of animal was that?"
- "What style of music is it?"

- "How would you tape a whale singing?"
- "Where does it come from?"
- "How did the whales and musicians work together?"
- "Were they whales or dolphins?"
- "How do you know if it was singing or talking?"
- "Why did they make the music with the animals?"

The types of questions the students shared showed aspects of their personalities and their individual intelligences (for more on Gardner's intelligences, refer to chapter 1). For example, Julien, who was particularly interested in math, wondered about the patterns that repeated in the music. Amber, who loves to dance, asked, "What type of rhythm were they using?" The wide variety of questions that emerged allowed us to discuss the different aspects of the music. For the students, this variety illustrated how questioning can go beyond vocabulary, allowing them to understand the intent and structure of the piece as well. An added bonus of this lesson was that as teachers, we did not have to model all the different types of questions. Because of the complexity and interpretive nature of music, the students easily developed a rich list of questions. Also, students realized that not all their questions could be answered.

The students were thrilled with the discussion. They loved asking questions, and many students wanted to share more than just one. Tapping into their excitement, we began the next part of the lesson to see if the students would be able to transfer this questioning to text.

While they were still gathered in a circle, Sabine read aloud a book about whales (any book on the general history of whales is appropriate) and encouraged the students to ask questions. Because we had used a piece of music with whales singing, the students already had prior knowledge of the subject. At the end of each paragraph, Sabine stopped reading in order to give students a chance to ask questions. Roberta noted the questions on chart paper. For example, students asked,

- "How could whales walk on land?"
- "Where did they find the skeletons of the animals?"
- "What part of the animal would be used to walk on the land?"
- "Do you think they used their fins to walk?"

We were pleased that without prompting, students were able to come up with such relevant questions.

The following day, we planned to give students 20 minutes to work independently on books they wanted to read. We passed out packets of sticky notes to students to mark passages in which they had questions. Then, we asked them to find comfortable places to read so they could spend all 20 minutes focused on their books. Some students curled up by the window or under desks, whereas others nestled in corners with pillows. When the 20 minutes were up, we were happy to see that each student had a few sticky notes marking passages in their books and that many students had at least one on every page. Students were excited to share their questions with the class. We asked them to share only the one or two questions that they felt were the most important. The following provides a sampling of some of the students' questions:

Roger: Why did the author put a strawberry on that page? It gives the story away.

Carter: How do clams get pearls in their mouths?

Jonathan: Why would a shark eat armor?

Allison: Why did this kid always want to do the opposite?

Jonas: In this contest, why don't boys ever win?

Elizabeth: Why are crabs scared of people?

One girl in our class, Jessie, particularly surprised us with her question. Jessie has multiple learning challenges and usually was not able to participate in our discussions. She was often silent and seldom able to follow the flow of a conversation and give input. During this exercise, however, Jessie had read a book about superheroes and formed a question related to the text. She announced to the class, "Why does Superman fly?"

It was apparent from these questions that the students had transferred their learning without sacrificing the quality of the questions. They asked questions about the author's intent, pieces of information that did not seem relevant to the text as a whole, and deeper themes they noticed in a story. These were the types of questions for which we had hoped. Although we were thrilled that the students had started to use the strategy, we knew that in order to build a deep and dynamic understanding of the strategy, it was important for them to keep working with it. Therefore, twice a week for the next three weeks, we used lessons to expand the students' use of questioning while reading. Each time, we used a different art form to develop the strategy further. Incorporating new art forms allowed the students to remain engaged and enthusiastic throughout these lessons, and allowed us to address a broader range of learning styles.

Throughout this month-long study on questioning, it became apparent that students understood questioning and had learned how to use this as a reading comprehension strategy. We observed students using questioning in a variety of reading contexts, such as during read-aloud, in small-group discussions, and when writing responses to stories. For example, during a read-aloud of *John Muir, Young Naturalist* (Dunham, 1975/1998), one passage described how Muir had brought along a bearskin during a winter camping trip. One student, Alex, quickly raised her hand and said, "I have a question. If John Muir says he loves nature so much, then why would he use a bearskin for his blanket?" Then, on a field trip later that week, as we passed some new urban development surrounded by small farms, Elise asked, "What do you think John Muir would be thinking about all this?" We were delighted that these types of questions became a common occurrence in book discussions, field trips, and class studies. Having these students use questioning to move through a piece of text and clarify the author's intent clearly expanded their reading comprehension.

Art-Based Lessons for Teaching Questioning

Using a Famous Piece of Artwork to Introduce Questioning

Grades: K–6

Artwork Resource: *Thirty-six Views of Mount Fuji: The Great Wave off Kanagawa* (Hokusai, 1830) or another quality painting or print

Lesson: We began this lesson by having the second-grade students sit in a circle, each with paper and a pencil. Next, we explained that they would be studying a wood-block print and writing down any questions related to the print. The students were eager to start, especially because we had turned the print toward the wall. One student, Allison, kept creeping over to peek, and another student, Manny, shouted, "Show us the picture!" We showed the class the print, *Thirty-six Views of Mount Fuji: The Great Wave off Kanagawa*, which shows two groups of men seated in hand-carved canoes and paddling through a giant wave. The students first sat silently looking at it and then started crawling forward to inspect its details. After they settled down from the initial excitement, we passed around the print. Once the students had a closer look, they wrote down questions the picture had generated.

After students finished writing their questions, we asked them to share their thoughts. Some examples follow:

- "Why would someone go out on a stormy night?"
- "What is that mountain at the back of the painting?"
- "Why would the artist have the boat going through the waves?"
- "How come all the people are in the back of the boat?"
- "What caused the storm?"

Reflection: This print helped stimulate the building of a mental construct around the topic of questioning. By offering another venue for questioning—art rather than text—students generated a multitude of questions as they deliberated about the artist's purpose. This was the type of questioning we wanted students to use to help them understand books they were reading. After we discussed the print and students' questions further, the students formed book groups based on various reading levels to think about similar types of questions for their books.

Using Movement to Develop Questioning About Text Structure

Grades: 2–4

Text Resource: "Long Trip" from *The Dream Keeper and Other Poems* (Hughes, 1994a)

Lesson: In this lesson, we used movement to help second-grade students develop questions about Hughes's poem "Long Trip," which describes a sea voyage. We started by writing the poem, which describes the movement of the sea, on the chalkboard for all to see. The whole class then read aloud the poem together. Following this reading, we asked the students to stand up in a circle and create movements for all the different phrases within the poem. The kids jumped to their feet, ready to begin. At first, only a few students raised their hands to volunteer a movement. One student, Elizabeth, suggested that we start with our hands across our chest and our feet together. Everyone seemed to agree that this was a good beginning. Then, for the line "the sea is a wilderness of waves" (p. 16), Bradley suggested that we move one arm from the far right to the left, making the shape of small waves. Once we started moving, more students added their ideas. Soon, we had motions for the whole poem. When we had all the movements for the poem, we practiced the whole piece. Figure 9 shows students as they move to the line "We dip and dive" (p. 16).

Each movement was a kinesthetic reminder of a particular phrase in the poem. Once the students had demonstrated a level of fluency with both the

Figure 9   Students "Dip and Dive" as They Move to "Long Trip"

words and movements of the poem, we stopped and had them ask questions. There were a number of questions about specific lines of the poem, such as "How would a boat dip and dive?" As students answered one another's questions, they referred to the movements they had created. Having that physical response to the vocabulary helped the students gain the meaning of the poem.

Reflection: As the students participated in this lesson, they noticed points in which their movements and the poem did not match because the author had played with the words. At these points, it became obvious that the students' movements encouraged them to ponder the author's intent and the poem's structure. As they struggled to make their movements match the changes in the poem, they were forced to think deeply about the author's intent.

Also, we observed that for kinesthetic learners, exploring questioning through movement helped add to their understanding of the strategy of questioning. As the dancer Isadora Duncan (as cited in Cornett, 1998) once said, "If I could tell you what I mean, there would be no point in dancing" (p. 286).

Using Construction to Introduce Questioning

Grades: K–3

Materials: blocks; math manipulatives, such as pattern blocks and base ten blocks; other building materials

Text Resources: *Great Buildings* (Lynch, 1996) and other books about building

Day One Lesson: When Erin was teaching first grade, she decided to introduce the strategy of questioning to her students. Because of her interest in trying new teaching methods, she invited us into her classroom to help her. The first graders swarmed around the building materials we had gathered in baskets on the rug in the circle area. They were enticed by blocks; math manipulatives, such as Cuisenaire rods and base ten blocks; and any other wooden materials we were able to scrounge from classrooms in our building. We had decided to explore the idea of questioning through the art of construction. Over the years, we observed children using blocks to build houses, towers, and castles. Conversations during these times were always full of questions; therefore, construction seemed like a natural starting point to explore the strategy of questioning.

We began by showing the students a photograph of a child building with blocks. He is poised over a tower, ready to place the final block on it. We asked the students what this child might be thinking. They responded confidently, "He's wondering if the block will balance." When we told the children about this activity, it was clear they were enthusiastic about the prospect of building. Their first project was to build the tallest towers possible. We asked each student to work with a classmate and to be serious about communicating with his or her partner about the building. To demonstrate some aspects of this communication process, we modeled building a collaborative structure.

As the children began building, we sat next to them to listen to their conversations. Alex, who was using large building blocks, asked his partner, Molly, "Do you think this block will work here?" After agreeing to place the large block on top, Molly wondered, "Do you think our base is strong enough?" After moving on to observe Adam and Neala, we heard Adam ask, "Do you like this block this way? I think it will look like a parking lot with a tall tower." We then heard Luis, who was sitting next to us, ask his partner, "Do you think if we build a really thick base with a thinner top, it will have prettiness in it?" We continued observing throughout the day.

Reflection: We sensed that most of the children were able to use the questions to help them communicate about their buildings. Questions centered on which building materials to use, the appearance of the buildings, and buildings' structural qualities. One common question was, "Do you think the building will fall?" Through construction, the students understood that questions were not always asked to get a specific answer, but often to help focus the direction of the activity. We wanted students to use this type of questioning while they read in order to facilitate their comprehension.

To further the students' understanding of questioning, we asked them each to draw pictures of their towers and write one question they had used while building. (Figure 10 shows a pair of students engaged in this activity, as well as a sample of one student's drawing and question.) In the discussion that followed, we listed the students' questions on the chalkboard and then sorted out which questions helped them build better. When the activity ended, the children asked if they could find books about different kinds of buildings to help them with their next building project.

Figure 10
First Graders Drawing and Writing Questions and Sample of Troy's Drawing and Question

Name: Troy   Date: May 15

Draw a picture of your building

Write down on question you had:

Was it going to. Fal?

Was it going to fall?

Day Two Lesson: The next morning, we decided to read a passage we had paraphrased from the book *Great Buildings*. The passage describes some unique building shapes, such as a building shaped like a bowl and museums with spiral staircases that seem to wind up into the sky without supports. We asked children to let us know if they had questions about the text as we read the passage, which we had copied on chart paper so everyone could see it. As the children asked questions—"How can you build in the shape of a bowl?" "Won't the staircase fall down?"—we recorded these on sticky notes and placed them on the chart paper.

The second building project followed, and we gave the children the same directions we had used for the first project. Following our modeling of a more intricate building, the students looked through books, marked their questions with sticky notes, and tried to create the most interesting building they could. Students were enthusiastic about the building, asking one another about pictures they had seen in books, experimenting with different blocks, and discussing whether certain building styles were beautiful. Their buildings became more detailed and elaborate.

Once these buildings were complete, children chose books from their book clubs to read independently. As usual, sticky notes were available for marking their questions. Throughout the actual building process, we noticed that Xiao, who is from China and new to our school, was more solitary and ended up building side by side with his partner. Yet his drawing of the building was detailed, and he recorded concrete questions. Because of his limited knowledge of the English language, we wondered if Xiao would be able to transfer this questioning to text. As he moved on to independent reading, however, Xiao surprised us by being full of questions about his book on what birds eat. He wondered, for example, "How can the bird eat a whole starfish," "How did that frog jump into the bird's mouth," and "This is a small bird: How can it eat a lizard?"

Reflection: Through our lesson on construction, we observed that students learning English as a second language can benefit from arts experiences even if they seem reluctant. Moreover, it seemed that the arts gave Xiao an opportunity to listen, watch, and participate in a nonthreatening atmosphere while developing an understanding of the strategy before working with text.

We found that construction was a fascinating topic for all children when they were given opportunities to experiment with their own theories. The children easily saw how certain questions led to more complex buildings, whereas other questions did not affect the building at all. Similarly, they began to see how certain questions led to understanding of more complex text.

Using Calligraphy to Develop Questioning About a Cultural Event

Grades: 4–5

Materials: calligraphy pens, ink, paper

Text Resources: *The House of Wisdom* (Heide & Gilliland, 1999) and *Masterpieces of the J. Paul Getty Museum: Illuminated Manuscripts* (Kren, 1997)

Lesson: *The House of Wisdom* is a captivating book set during the ninth century in the city of Baghdad, Iraq. During this period, Europe was going through the Dark Ages, while the caliph of Baghdad was collecting and translating manuscripts of ancient philosophers from around the world. We used this book during the fourth graders' study of medieval history. Our students were eager to study calligraphy, having recently mastered handwriting. We thought that the quiet, focused work of learning calligraphy, as well as the intricate forms of the Old English alphabet, would help them empathize with the young character in *The House of Wisdom*. Calligraphy was meant to bridge the gap of time and distance, thus enabling the children to ask meaningful questions about the text. Indeed, students gained expertise in calligraphy as they questioned the flow of ink and their ability to form letters.

We began this lesson by sharing with the class some pages of *Illuminated Manuscripts*, which has pictures of beautiful illuminated manuscripts. Illuminated works come from medieval books that monks spent hours decorating with rich detail, color, and gold leaf. Spontaneous questions abounded such as, "Is that really gold?" and "Is that writing?" As they looked at each new page, the students loved trying to figure out which letter was hidden in the detailed drawing at the beginning of the page. Students wanted to use calligraphy to make their medieval stories, which they would compose in writing workshop, more beautiful. Energy filled the room as we passed out copies of the calligraphy alphabet and pens: The students could not wait to try their hands at this style of handwriting. After students finished writing their stories, they began to illuminate their pieces. However, students' energy dissipated as they began to struggle with the complexity of the task. Although many were discouraged by the amount of time it took, most students were at least able to use an illuminated letter at the beginning of their stories for writing workshop (see Figure 11). Once some of the manuscripts were completed, we used author's chair at the end of writing workshop to give students a chance to share their stories. As we listened to students' comments, it became apparent that they viewed these stories as treasured pieces of writing because of all the hard work involved in their creation.

Figure 11 Students' Illuminated Letters

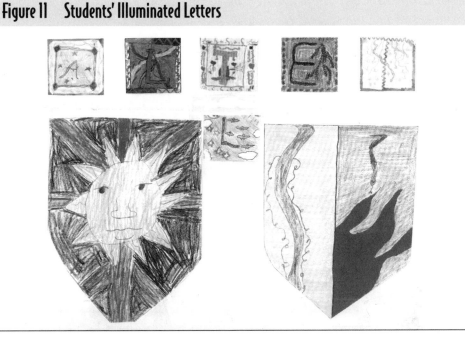

When the students read *The House of Wisdom*, their questions centered on the precious nature of the ancient manuscripts that the caliph saves and on the insight of the people who work so hard to save them. As we had hoped, they developed an appreciation of the time and talent it took for the young character in this book to copy a manuscript.

Reflection: The discussion that followed the reading of this text made it apparent to us that by working on their own illuminated manuscripts, students were able to experience struggles similar to the young character. For example, Michael went through a small stack of paper before he was happy with his title page. The students also experienced the pride that came with accomplishing a difficult task. This prior experience gave students the ability to generate meaningful questions about the text rather than wait for teacher-initiated questions. We realized that by using the arts, the students had stronger motivation to understand a piece of writing, which in turn, generated thought-provoking questions.

Using Mask Making to Develop Questioning About Character

Grades: 4–5

Materials: plaster strips (can be purchased at a pharmacy); Vaseline; acrylic or tempera paint; paintbrushes; feathers, glitter, and other objects for decoration

Text Resources: *The Cay* (Taylor, 1969), *Snow Treasure* (McSwigan, 1942), and *Number the Stars* (Lowry, 1989)

Lesson: The fifth-grade students were reading books about World War II—*The Cay, Snow Treasure,* and *Number the Stars*. A major theme in all these books is the difference between how people view themselves and how others view these people. We thought this theme would lead to many questions about why people stereotype one another. The process of creating masks seemed to be a natural way to encourage students to ask more complex questions about this theme.

Once students made the plaster masks (see Appendix B for specifics on this arts technique), they painted the masks on the outside to show how others viewed them. The students then painted or wrote a poem on the inside of the masks that reflected how they viewed themselves. This activity prodded the students to ask questions about the discrepancies between the two sides of the mask.

The next time students met in their book groups to discuss the books they were reading, we gave each group a large piece of tagboard shaped like a mask. We asked each group to choose one of the main characters in the story that group was reading and make a mask similar to the ones they had made of themselves. Before making the masks, the groups first discussed the characters. We observed students' conversations as they questioned one another about characters and how others viewed those characters. Because of the sensitive material in these books, there were many heated conversations. For example, the group reading *Number the Stars* debated why some people could treat the Jewish people so horribly, whereas other people were willing to risk their lives to save them. One student in this group wondered how the group could represent both views on the front of the mask. After creating a list of internal and external characteristics, each group began creating its character mask.

Reflection: As we monitored the groups' discussions, we noticed that the questions students asked revolved around larger social themes, such as discrimination and prejudice. It was apparent that having students first question their own beliefs about who they were added depth to the questions they had about characters in the books.

Using Movement to Develop Questioning About Nonfiction Text

Grades: K–2

Text Resources: *Under the Sea from A to Z* (Doubilet, 1991) and nonfiction books about Australian animals (any will work well)

Music Resource: any recorded didgeridoo music (a didgeridoo is a long hollow bamboo or wooden tube of Australian Aboriginal origin; blowing on one end of the tube creates different sounds depending on the vibrations)

Lesson: In this lesson, we decided to use movement to help first-grade students develop questions about Australian animals. The students had been reading nonfiction books about Australian animals that they had chosen to study. We thought that by having the students become their animals, they would develop deeper understanding of what they already knew, which would then help them refine the questions they had about their animals.

Before we began, we asked students to move their desks to one side of the classroom. We then told each to pretend to be the animal that he or she was studying. As the didgeridoo music played, we asked students to move to the music the way they thought their animals would. We prompted students to move in specific ways with questions such as "How would your animal dig a hole," "How would it swim," "How would it run," and "How would it sleep?" In response to one question, Mike explained, "I am a snake. I can't dig a hole." After trying a series of different movements together, we gathered the students and recorded their questions as they shared them with the class. The movement activity produced a wide range of questions such as "If my animal can't dig a hole, how could they live there?" and "I wonder how a koala sleeps?"

Next, Sabine read *Under the Sea From A to Z*, an alphabet book about sea creatures. We reminded students of all the interesting questions they had about animals during the previous activity and asked them to use the same type of thinking while we read the book and recorded their questions. There was a slight buzz in the room when they heard about the leafy sea dragon, so we let everyone share his or her question. In order to finish the book, we had to limit the number of questions to two per page.

Reflection: By pretending to be Australian animals, the students had to think about what they already knew about the animals. This led to puzzlement when we asked students to create an unusual movement for their specific animals. It seemed as if the gap between what they did and did not know opened students to new questions. While reading aloud the book, we noticed that one provocative question often led to a second. Although the book did not have answers to all the students' questions, having the chance to ask these questions deepened their comprehension of the topic.

Final Thoughts

This chapter demonstrated how the arts were able to break down barriers for students, such as Jessie and Xiao. When questioning text, students time and again feel that there must be the perfect question to ask. However, this was seldom the case when students tried to construct the tallest building, pondered how to form beautiful handwriting, or created masks about characters. When students engaged in those types of activities, they overflowed with questions. Questioning should feel like a natural interaction with the world. We discovered that the arts allowed a broad range of students to understand the power of questioning as a reading comprehension strategy.

Chapter 5

Determining Importance

Art is the lie that enables us
to realize the truth.

—Pablo Picasso (as cited in Cornett, 1998, p. 190)

Children in Sabine's fourth-grade class gather on the floor of the art room with Licia, her student teacher. Licia has taped to the chalkboard Pablo Picasso's series of drawings depicting a bull from *Picasso: Art Activity Pack* (Boutan, 1998). The drawings show Picasso's progression of work from a realistic sketch with many details to a simple figure with only three lines. Licia asks the students, "Which drawing do you think Picasso started with?" A chorus of students call out "the stick figure," the drawing with the least amount of detail. Licia responds, "What would you think if I told you that he started with the drawing with the most detail?" Students ponder this for a moment. One student, Benza, exclaims, "He's taking parts away!" Students then begin to reflect on the process. Jennifer finally says, "Oh, he's only leaving what's really important!" Licia explains how artists often deconstruct a scene in order to highlight what is most significant and asks, "So how is this like reading?" Liam responds, "When you read, you have to figure out what's most important, too."

What Is Determining Importance?

Determining importance in text is about figuring out what is essential. Readers need to understand the most important ideas the author is trying to convey, such as the most important concepts about characters. Readers also need to gather critical information for their research. However, determining importance is often difficult for readers because they can be distracted by the amount and variety of interesting details. Readers can miss what is important in a text.

We wanted to help students think deeply about the important messages authors intend to convey in their text. Also, we wanted to give students a variety of formats to determine importance so they could fine-tune their ability to spot the essentials in the text. Learning about the artistic process allowed students to discover how artists make decisions about what details to focus on and what details to ignore. We saw this format as important in helping students learn to distinguish between the details of a text and the primary message of a text.

Children learn to find the essence of text when given a broad variety of formats and expression. For many children, the ability to focus on the important ideas comes more easily when given the opportunity to act out the story or visually represent the ideas. The arts provide visible mental constructs that encourage exploration and critical thinking, as well as an intense engagement with text.

Using the Arts to Teach Determining Importance

When we embarked on our project, we asked ourselves what it was about the arts that made a difference for some children in reading comprehension. We now believe that the arts give children an opportunity to use their many intelligences to construct new interpretations of text. Children discovered the ability to create new insights when using a kinesthetic or visual approach to understand text.

The arts also provided a social experience that allowed for discussions, arguments, and negotiations that produced new levels of thinking for some children. As a group, they were in the process of creating meaning from text. Research in drama and language arts shows that children make new connections around the meaning of narrative when they deal with different points of view (Wagner, 1998). Drama also lets students live through a moment in time as if it were their own. During these moments, a child's imagination can inform his or her critical thinking.

Further, we found that other forms of art, such as a poem or a song, offered a specific structure to point students toward essential ideas. Indeed, a common role of the arts in culture is pointing the way toward important ideas. We used the arts, therefore, to scaffold children's expression of ideas, and often to give them a model to follow.

Studies reported by Eric Jensen in *Arts With the Brain in Mind* (2001) show that children who participate in music lessons score higher on spatial reasoning tests than other children. In other words, these children are more capable of putting the pieces together into a whole. The arts seemed to help our students accomplish the same—supporting them in taking the parts of a text and creating a visual image that led to an understanding of the whole idea.

An In-Depth Look at Teaching How to Determine Importance Through Drama

Third graders were reading *The King's Equal* (Paterson, 1999), which is a short chapter book of a modern story written as a fairy tale. The book deals with a prince who, in order to receive his father's crown and become the true king, must find a wife who is his equal in wealth, intelligence, and beauty. The woman he finally finds, Rosamund, shows these qualities in surprising ways. Rosamund's friends include two small goats and a magical wolf.

Students began each day by reading part or all of a chapter. We decided to ask the children to create double-entry journals in which they wrote details on one side of the page and the main ideas on the other side of the same page. We asked students to write about what seemed most important in the text using the format we gave them. Not surprising, most children wrote about details of the story rather than the major themes.

Because this group of third graders meets for only 45 minutes four times a week, we looked for a way to use drama that would take a shorter amount of time but still reap its benefits. The idea of using tableaux interested us because they had some of the same elements of drama but required that children develop an idea through movements and gestures. As previously noted, to create a tableau, students use their bodies to produce a frozen scene of gestures and images that focus on an idea or event from the text. Although dialogue about the text is crucial, there is no actual talking in a tableau. Within a series of tableaux depicting a text, the final tableau is like a still-life photo: Students create a scene that shows the essence of the text. (See Appendix B for specifics on the technique of a tableau.)

We began our work by talking about stance and gesture. As we discussed where and how each character would stand, it was as if we were blocking a scene for a play. We talked about how each character could show what was happening in the scene with a body gesture or facial expression. We later taught students about how a variety of levels add interest to a tableau. Occasionally, students were allowed to use one or two simple props. Although props and costumes are not necessary for a tableau and may even get in the way, we sometimes used them to encourage children's ability to enter into the story world. Props support children in putting on the role of a character without adding specificity. Simple silk capes from a local toy store seem to work well as costumes in any play and are easy to use and store. The capes we purchased for students' tableaux came in a variety of rich colors and fabrics.

While children were designing their tableaux, we asked questions. This became an essential part of our work together because it helped children clarify their thinking. We would ask questions such as "How will you show that the prince is arrogant," "How can the wolf challenge the prince," and "What would Rosamund hold in her hand to show she is industrious?" Because we believed that there were many ways to reach the main idea in the story and that there would be many variations on the main idea, we carefully used these questions to follow up on the students' thinking rather than to introduce our own ideas.

When students reached their desired tableaux, we took a photo of each tableau with a digital camera. This photo gave students immediate feedback on their work. Figure 12 shows Grace and Serina in the process of creating two tableaux to express Rosamund's kindness to the magical wolf. At first, students thought this was the important part of the story, but they later discovered that it was only one of the interesting details.

Figure 12   Grace and Serina Create Tableaux for *The King's Equal*

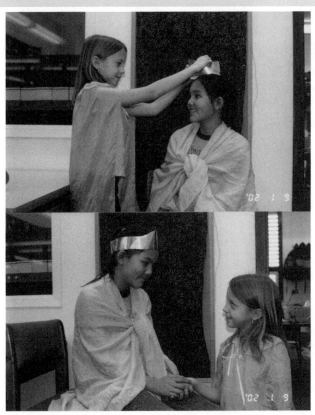

After taking pictures of each tableau, we rephrased our questions about the most important themes in the chapter. This time, children responded with more in-depth thinking about the text. Using gestures and facial expressions to tell parts of the story helped them decide what they should consider portraying from the text and what they should disregard. It was as if they had found a way to highlight the important parts of the text with their movements and gestures instead of with their writing.

We wondered aloud to the children about how their ability to find essential ideas changed so dramatically after building tableaux. They answered, "We can *see* it now!" One student, Theodore, said, "When we do a tableau, I feel it in my body, then the idea comes to my head." Patricia added, "That happens to me when I draw pictures from books at home."

The construction of a scene in the physical sense helped students see the wholeness of the many concepts being presented in the text. The photograph of each tableau was always a pleasure for them to see, but it was clearly the creation of the tableaux that supported their thinking, and there was no difference in their level of work when the photograph was missing. The work of Bell (1991) points to some reasoning behind the success of drama and tableau. She states that in order to comprehend a passage of text, readers need to be able to visualize what the words are telling them. Many readers do this automatically. But some readers have a concept-imagery disorder that prevents them from automatically creating a visualization; however, they can be taught to visualize text. This is where drama and tableaux play an important role in reading—creating the visual image so students can imagine the whole of the text.

Another benefit of using drama and tableau was that they gave children the opportunity to use their bodies to organize their thinking. For children whose primary intelligence is kinesthetic, learning that included physical movement supported their particular learning method. We also saw this occur when these children used other forms of movement, such as dancing the water cycle or creating a model of the digestive system with their classmates.

Art-Based Lessons for Determining Importance

Using Poetry to Highlight How Important Details Support Central Themes

Grades: K–5

Materials: natural materials, such as shells, rocks, and pine cones, or mechanical objects, such as an eggbeater or a coffee grinder, for viewing

Text Resources: *The Important Book* (Brown, 1949) and nonfiction books that create mental images, such as *The Last Wild Edge: One Woman's Journey From the Arctic Circle to the Olympic Rain Forest* (Zwinger, 1999) and *New and Selected Poems* (Oliver, 1992)

Lesson: We decided to explore this strategy with third graders in our struggling-reader group. The four students in this group—Georgia, Pat, Tobias, and Daniel—met with us every morning to read, write, and discuss books together. They made up a lively group that took some energy to hold together and focus, but they loved stories and wanted to read better.

Before the group began reading *The Important Book*, we modeled the strategy of determining importance. We showed them ways to use details to build a description of an object, by reading passages from nonfiction books that created unique images of natural objects. From *New and Selected Poems*, we chose to read the poem "The Summer Day," which provides a beautiful description of grasshoppers. The students also listened to a passage from Susan Zwinger's book that describes ravens as they "leap, hop, wrestle, preen, and flop on the banks of the Ross River among the wind-stirred yellow leaves" (p. 28). Then, Roberta read *The Important Book*, a book-length poem, to show the students how the format of a poem was useful in sorting out key ideas and details. The following excerpt about wind provides a sampling of this poem:

> The important thing about wind
> is that it blows.
> You can't see it,
> but you can feel it on your cheek,
> and see it bend trees,
> and blow hats away,
> and sail boats.
> But the important thing about wind
> is that it blows. (n.p.)

Afterward, the children looked at several tools and natural objects and attempted to name important qualities about them, as well as other interesting details they observed. After students looked at a large smooth stone and each had a chance to hold it in his or her hands, Roberta asked them to attempt to organize their thoughts about the stone, the way Brown had organized her thoughts in the poems. The following excerpt is an example of one student's poem:

The most important about a rock
is that it's part of nature
rocks can be smooth or rough
rocks can be boulders or pebbles
rocks can be speckled or full of crystals
but the most important thing about a rock
is that it's part of nature

Finally, we showed students the school's new digital camera. They were interested in how it worked, so they examined it. We took pictures of the students, then they drew pictures of the camera using black-ink line drawings. We asked the group to use the same format as the author to write about the importance of cameras. Two students, Georgia and Pat, wrote the following poem together:

The most important thing about
a camera is that it takes the
moments of your life and keeps
them forever so you can remember
when you were a baby so you
can remember when you were in
kindergarten so you can remember
when you had a best friend the
important thing about a camera is
that it takes the moments of your
live [sic] and keeps them forever

Reflection: We sensed that the children were beginning to grasp the distinction between descriptive details and central themes, as they used details to build a picture of an object with an emphasis on which details were most important. The format of poetry is crisp and to the point but also may involve pattern and repetition. The format of Brown's poems, therefore, gave our students a sense of how to support a major theme with important details.

Using Process Drama to Determine Importance in Nonfiction Text

Grades: 4–5

Text Resource: ...If You Lived in Colonial Times (McGovern, 1992)

Lesson: When Erin first came to our school, she taught the fifth-grade class. As part of a history study, she invited us to work with children who were struggling with determining importance. Erin's class was studying the American colonial period, and she had organized historical-fiction book clubs based on students' reading levels. She wanted us to meet with a group of bright, articulate boys who were reluctant readers.

We thought the book ...*If You Lived in Colonial Times* would appeal to them because the nonfiction format was interesting and easy to read. But the students came to our first meeting without their books and with sparsely written notes in their double-entry journals. The boys had studied the structure of nonfiction and had learned how to use double-entry journals and sticky notes to mark important passages. Even though Erin had given them a foundation for working with text, they continued to struggle. The boys were engrossed in the particulars of colonial schools such as the dunce cap, cold rooms, and hard benches. We realized that many students remembered history by its fascinating details rather than its significant themes.

We started our work with this group knowing that the boys' learning style was primarily kinesthetic. Therefore, we decided to use process drama as a format to help them think about and articulate important issues. Process drama is an improvisational style of drama that focuses more on problem solving than performance (see Appendix B for specifics on the technique of process drama). Dialogue is impromptu, as children become the characters from the text. We often introduce these dramas by beginning with a letter that indicates there is a problem within the context of our current discussion. Through the process drama, students should try to resolve the problem. So we gave the boys a few props and the following letter:

> You have been enrolled in Master Sniffert's morning class at the schoolhouse on Pine Bough Road. He will be expecting you on the 15th day of the month of October. Bring one armful of firewood, a new slate, and two pieces of chalk. Be prompt. You will be on probation for three months until we are certain that the behavior you displayed at your former school does not resurface here.

We watched as the boys role-played and began to pull out the core ideas of colonial school life. Erin entered the drama in a role as one of the students. She was able to create the dramatic conflict by asking the questions the other students needed to verbally respond to, enabling them to sort through important ideas and create generalizations.

In the discussion that followed the drama, the students articulated their insights about what school was really like in the 18th century—it was uncomfortable, it was strict, it was based on humiliation and shame. We had a much more focused conversation than we had 30 minutes earlier.

Reflection: During this process drama, students actively engaged in creating meaning, not just receiving information. This type of activity required students to question, respond, and deal with information as if it was real and in the present. Dorothy Heathcote, a drama educator from England, and Gavin Bolton (1995) write, "Thinking from within the situation immediately forces a different kind of thinking" (p. vii). While students are engaged in drama, thinking from within the situation helps them identify important ideas.

Using a Sand Tray to Organize Important Ideas Visually

Grades: K–3

Materials: four pieces of wood 3" × 24"; one piece of flat board 24" × 24"; screws and a drill; fine sand; small figures of animals, people, and imaginary characters; small natural objects, such as shells, driftwood, jewels or stones, nuts, and pine cones

Text Resource: *The King's Equal* (Patterson, 1999)

Lesson: During the reading of the final chapter of *The King's Equal* with our third-grade book club, mentioned earlier in the chapter, we decided to use our sand tray to create a visual image of the book's important ideas (see Appendix B for specifics on creating sand trays). This is an important activity for students who have difficulty with reading comprehension, because it allows them to build stories before they talk or write about them. We wanted our book club to transition their visualizing skills into visualizing the book's main ideas. We hoped that if the students built the model in the sand tray, it would be a step toward more independence: Eventually, they would use these skills automatically to visualize what the words were telling them.

After reading about the prince's transformation into a kind person who befriends the wolf, the students built a model of the prince, the wolf, and the goats sitting around a fire, telling stories, and baking bread. Building this model and others allowed the students to become increasingly able to identify the main ideas in their writing, as well.

We then asked them to read passages from the book and make mental pictures of the models, imagining the stance and gesture of the characters, as well as the props. At the end of this lesson, the children thought the author's intent was to show how the prince changed in the story. Their sand-tray model of the prince as the new king, baking his own bread over the fire, symbolized the prince's change (see Figure 13).

Reflection: Our time together in this book club was charged by the children's enthusiasm. Their engagement in their work showed us how compelling this integration of the arts was for them; they literally begged for more

time in book club. It also was apparent that the work the children did with concrete materials helped them make their ideas more concrete. This ability gave them confidence as they talked about the meaning of text. An abstract concept such as transformation became filled with meaning for the children as they worked with tangible materials that helped represent the concept.

Using Portrait Painting to Model Determining Importance

Grades: 2–5

Materials: oil pastels, watercolor paints, paintbrushes, heavy-duty drawing paper or watercolor paper, permanent black markers

Text Resource: *My Heroes, My People: African Americans and Native Americans in the West* (Monceaux & Katcher, 1999)

Lesson: We furthered our study of determining importance in text by communicating the importance of paintings to the second-grade students, who were studying heroes. We used Morgan Monceaux's passionate portraits in *My Heroes, My People,* which contains a mix of paintings and collage, to illustrate this importance. The children loved these portraits, which all have a bit of writing around the shoulders and faces of their subjects. The students wondered aloud about how the author decided what to write there. As Roberta read this writing, it seemed that the children began to understand how determining importance was unique for each person. They also thought about how it depended on the intended audience and the author's purpose for writing.

After reading this book, Roberta asked each child to choose a hero for the subject of his or her portrait painting (see Appendix B for specifics on portrait painting). When students completed their portraits, they used a watercolor wash over the entire portrait to add vibrancy. Then, children chose the most important thing they wanted to communicate about their heroes and wrote it with a permanent black marker around the edge of the shoulders and head of their portraits' subject. Similar to Monceaux, they had to make decisions about what was essential to write around the edges of their portraits. See Figure 14 for Chandra's portrait of Martin Luther King, Jr.

Figure 14   Chandra's Portrait of Martin Luther King, Jr.

Reflection: As the children worked on completing their portraits, we observed them taking the job of determining importance very seriously. The task of writing the essential idea about the subject around the portrait helped cement this strategy in their minds because it was a visual reminder of how what is essential needs to stand out for readers in some form. We have found the same success when using this activity during nonfiction research with older students, by asking them to paint a picture of an animal they had studied and write an essential idea around the edge of the picture.

Using Quilting to Develop Symbols for Important Ideas

Grades: 2–5

Materials for Paper Quilts: one piece of butcher paper large enough to accommodate each student's pattern block and glue, and for each student, four 3-inch right triangles in bright colors and one 6-inch square in a contrasting color or pattern

Materials for Fabric Quilts: scissors, backing fabric that is slightly larger than the finished quilt top, batting for the middle of the quilt, 2.5-inch fabric strips for borders between squares (number of strips needed will depend on the number of squares), and for each student, four 3-inch right triangles in bright colors, one 6-inch square of fabric in a contrasting color or pattern, one needle and thread, four 3-inch right triangles of fabric adhesive

Text Resources: *Follow the Drinking Gourd* (Winter, 1988), *Hidden in Plain View: A Secret Story of Quilts and the Underground Railroad* (Tobin & Dobard, 1999), and *Zlata's Diary: A Child's Life in Sarajevo* (Filipovic, 1994)

Lesson: During a yearlong study of migration, third graders studied the movement of African Americans in the United States from the rural South to the cities of the North after the Civil War. We integrated this study and a geometry study with a quilt project called "Journey to Freedom."

First, students read *Follow the Drinking Gourd* and other stories of the African American migration, and we concentrated on not only the people's struggles but also their courage. Then, from the book *Hidden in Plain View*, we shared stories of how freed slaves used different quilt designs to send messages preparing those who were about to escape from slavery by way of the Underground Railroad. For example, a quilt design such as the monkey wrench might have let slaves know to pack up their tools. Or, if a quilt with the tumbling-blocks pattern was hung on a fence, it might have indicated that the time had come for the escape.

After these readings, the students decided they wanted to make a quilt of their own. We began with a paper quilt so children could easily make several paper patterns from which to choose as they decided which one depicted their image of the slaves' journey. We gave each student four right triangles that were placed in the four corners of a 6-inch square of a contrasting color (see Appendix B for specific directions on paper quilting, which also can be used as a jumping-off place for fabric quilting). Then, we asked students to visualize a pattern block using the triangles; they came up with 17 pattern variations. We glued students' pattern blocks on a large piece of butcher paper to make our class quilt.

Students also thought of words or phrases that described the images they saw in their patterns. For example, some patterns reminded them of trees, fences, or roads that slaves might have seen on their journey to freedom. Because all traditional quilt pattern blocks have names, the students also named their favorite pattern blocks in a way that reminded them of the journeys they had read about. These visual quilt patterns helped the students anchor important ideas from the journey stories we had read. We once again shared with students how African American quilts were "communicating secrets using ordinary objects" (Tobin & Dobard, 1999, p. 35), because we wanted students to use their own designs to focus on determining an important aspect of the journey to think about and share. More important, we wanted students to experience how images can be linked to language and thinking, enabling them to explore abstract ideas more easily. The discussion that coincided with our construction of the quilt helped children piece together the quilt and the story, respectively.

Next, we asked students to use their paper designs as the patterns for their fabric squares (see Appendix B for specific instructions on fabric quilting). Students chose fabric from our scrap bag, then cut their triangles and attached them to the squares using fabric adhesive. When they finished, one student's parent sewed together all the squares into one class quilt. We then asked each child to write a short poem to go with his or her square, describing his or her perceptions of African Americans' feelings and dreams as they made their incredible journey to the North. The writing that followed was some of their most pointed and heartfelt of the year.

A year later, as the same students read *Zlata's Diary: A Child's Life in Sarajevo* and talked about the Balkan conflict, one student raised his hand and pointed to the quilt on the wall. Showing his understanding of the concepts we had learned during our quilt project, he suggested that we send the refugees in Sarajevo our freedom quilt to give them hope.

Reflection: The process of creating a concrete piece of artwork with symbolic meaning helped the children think about the meaning within *Hidden in Plain View*. The quilt project was useful in generating ideas, as well as in sifting important ideas that helped the children really understand the importance that symbolism played in the story. Once again, the visualization gave students time and a focus for their thinking.

Using Fabric Collage and Poetry to Differentiate Important Ideas From Details

Grades: 3–5

Materials: fabric scraps (wrapping paper or paper with interesting designs also will work well if you do not have access to fabrics), fabric glue, scissors

Text Resources: *In the Hollow of Your Hand: Slave Lullabies* (McGill, 2000) and "Women" (Walker, 2001)

Lesson: We decided to use *In the Hollow of Your Hand* and Alice Walker's poem "Women," from *Words With Wings: A Treasury of African-American Poetry and Art*, to help fifth-grade girls learn more about determining importance. The artist of *In the Hollow of Your Hand*, Michael Cummings, uses fabric-quilt collages to express the beauty and longing of the lullabies in the book.

To begin, we pulled out a bag of fabric scraps that we had collected from parents and teachers for our collage. Showing the girls how each fabric had fascinating details, we explained that each piece would help build our collage. We also explained that one fabric should not dominate the picture, but rather each fabric should build on the other, so their choice of fabric was important. We showed the students how Cummings used a variety of fabrics to add detail to each collage but explained that all the fabrics expressed one important image or idea from the lullaby it depicted. To model this concept, we chose a lullaby from the book, "Lil Girl Sittin' in de Briar Bush," and showed students how the artist mixed both light and dark fabrics, subtle and lively fabrics, and many detailed fabrics in order to create a cohesive picture with a strong message. This process is similar to the process of determining importance in text, as the list of details leads readers to important ideas. We hoped the students would see this connection.

Next, we read Walker's poem "Women," which describes mothers as "husky of voice" and "stout of step" (n.p.) and as generals who fight battles so their children have what they need.

We then asked the girls to make their own collage and write a collective poem that would show the most important things about their own mothers. For several of our meetings together, the girls cut and glued together pieces of fabric until they had a cohesive whole of lively and subtle fabrics. Because they played together frequently, the girls' conversations during this time showed how well they knew one another's families. The girls wrote their poem after finishing their collage (see Figure 15). Although it predictably began with a laundry list of observations about their mothers, it proceeded to build toward important ideas, just as their collage had. Readers often see details first, but as long as they use their sense of pattern and design to put those details together to see the bigger picture, they will be able to know what is essential.

Reflection: It was clear that sorting through fabric scraps and creating a collage had helped the girls assimilate the important details and ideas of poetry. Grasping the essence of text and creating it in poetry is akin to the experience of creating an art piece—both are deeply satisfying. During the

Figure 15   Fifth-Grade Girls' Poem About Their Mothers

Our mothers are

Cooking
Cleaning
Washing

Holding our hands

Making us comfortable
Getting us ready for School
Wishing for us to clean up our
messes

Wishing for us
to Stop dawdling
Wishing for us to get an education
Wishing for us to be happy

creation of the collage, we asked the girls to choose fabrics that reminded them of their mothers. The spoke easily about their mothers' love of brightly colored clothes, jewelry, and fancy boots. Comparing different ideas about their mothers to different scraps of fabric helped the girls define for themselves the essential ideas about their mothers. Further, matching fabric to details of these descriptions helped the girls understand the importance of details in both the story and the collage.

As a group, it was challenging for the girls to show their main idea in their collage. The immediate visual feedback they received from the concrete piece of artwork helped them realize when they were using either too much or too little detail. The girls moved fabric on and off their collage until they believed their message was clear. For children who are kinesthetic learners, the ability to physically rearrange details of a story or message helps them organize their thinking more easily.

Using Songwriting to Determine Importance in Nonfiction Research

Grades: 1–5

Text Resource: *Crocodile Smile: 10 Songs of the Earth as the Animals See It* (Weeks, 1994)

Lesson: When we teach research with young children, we use songwriting as a way to help them highlight major themes. For example, we used songwriting to help first graders with research projects on animals of the rain forest. Each child chose an animal to learn more about, and we organized the questions children had about the animals in order to help them with their research. When children were ready to begin writing their projects, we introduced them to the song "Piece of Jungle," from *Crocodile Smile*. We used this song, about how the jungle provides a home to a multitude of animals, to demonstrate how songwriters sometimes use the chorus to summarize the song's main idea and how each verse may add details about the animal.

Lines repeated in the song such as "that's what jungle is—home" and "under same blue sky" (n.p.) helped children to see how this songwriting technique aided them in identifying the song's message. They then used this technique in their own writing about the rain forest. Their growing love for the rain forest emerged as a message they wanted to share with others, so we wrote a song together. This songwriting experience helped students see how details about Ben's howler monkey or Chandra's jaguar flowed into a chorus that identified the most important ideas about each animal.

Reflection: The format of songwriting helped the children think through the differences between descriptive details and essential elements of text. The model of a song, which they asked to sing repeatedly, gave them a chance to dwell on an idea, practice it, and create an innovation of the model for their own song. When they wrote their song, the children knew instinctively which phrases to use for the chorus lines. These incremental steps gave children the tools to learn how to discern important elements in text.

Final Thoughts

Comprehension is often best expressed by the ability of the reader to determine what is important in the text. This chapter showed how in narrative pieces, important themes identified by readers varied depending on what they brought to the reading in terms of their own interests and needs. In teaching nonfiction text, however, we assumed that there was significant learning that would be the same for each reader; therefore, we made the effort to help students listen for the author's voice and message in each piece but honored that each child's interests still defined his or her conclusions about the text.

Using the arts was critical to help students learn to determine importance, because it allowed students to work in their strongest intelligence—whether visual, musical, or kinesthetic—and recognize what was important in text more easily. We believe that the process of doing art helps children focus on highlighting the essential. Further, we think that "art gives shape and stability to the valued materials of life, in order that they may be stressed, attended to and preserved" (Miles, as cited in Cornett, 1998, p. 225). Creating art encouraged our students to ask the question, "What am I trying to communicate?" Choosing a fabric for a collage, a gesture for a tableau, or a line for a refrain of a song helped them determine the essential message of their artwork.

Source: Quinn, J. (1997). *Deaf* [Glazed terra cotta]. Private collection. Photo by Claire Garoutte

Chapter 6

Inferring

Art does not reproduce the visible;
rather it makes visible.

—Paul Klee (as cited in Andrews, 1993, p. 58)

The light catches the creamy rounded curve of the ceramic piece. It seems to hang delicately in the air. It is balanced, as if poised for movement. When looking at the piece, questions abound in your mind. Is it one object or two? How do they float? Is it an old or new piece? What is it about? And then thoughts start to settle, and ideas form around what the artist is trying to communicate to you, the viewer.

A moment later, you scan the border around the piece, and at the bottom right corner, you find the title—*Deaf*—and a whole new layer of meaning unfolds. No longer does it appear to be one object, as two distinct cups come into focus. Then you realize that these two cups have turned on each other and are no longer communicating. With this new understanding, a transformation occurs. Suddenly, you are brought into the artist's inner world. You now know more about what the artist is trying to convey to the audience. This new insight allows you to make new connections to your own life, perhaps reminding you of the uncomfortable feeling of a strained relationship with a parent or friend. During this experience, you used inferential thinking to create meaning about the artwork that was not explicitly there and thus, created a unique interpretation.

When ceramicist Jeanne Quinn, from the University of Colorado, first shared her work with us, we were astounded. Each piece, beautiful in its own being, brought us along on her personal journey. As she presented each new piece, we *oohed* and *aahed*. We took a moment to internalize the piece and then modify our thoughts about it as she told us the title and story behind the piece of art. Throughout this experience, we continually used inferring to find meaning in art and to expand our thinking about each piece.

At an early age, many people develop methods of gaining meaning from art, often relying on inference only. Without being aware of it, people make inferences all the time when they experience art—whether looking at a painting, watching a dance performance, listening to a piece of music, or reading a book. Because of this basic connection, the arts lend themselves to being strong platforms for teaching the strategy of inferring. Through connecting, elaborating on, and teaching inferential thinking with the arts, we were able to reach a wide range of learners. Regardless of their current levels of learning, almost all students were able to participate in the art lessons and develop the strategic thinking necessary to become competent readers.

What Is Inferring?

Inferring is critical to a reader's ability to comprehend and enjoy text. As previously noted, inferring never happens in isolation because it weaves the reader's prior knowledge, connections, questions, and predictions and the author's information and summaries into a personal tapestry of understanding. Inferring requires that readers use their own perspectives of the world to help clarify and gain meaning from the text. This process enables readers to develop a uniquely personal understanding of the text. Inferring is also one of the most complex reading comprehension strategies. The common expression "reading between the lines" often holds little meaning for children, but good readers must learn to move beyond the obvious but still stay focused on the text.

The manner in which readers use inferring differs depending on the purpose. For example, while reading a fiction piece, readers may depend more on their own prior knowledge than they do when they read a nonfiction piece. As we thought about how to help our students develop inferential thinking, two main aspects of inferring emerged. The first aspect involves the personal side of inferring that occurs when readers make assumptions and form opinions about the meaning of text based on their prior knowledge. However, we both had experienced talking with children about the meaning of a book and getting responses that seemed connected to the text but actually added little to the children's deeper understanding of the book. For instance, when discussing a book in which the main character is a dog, a student raised his hand and shared, "I have a dog, too." Although the book obviously touched on the student's prior knowledge, he was not sharing a new insight about the book. Our first goal, then, was to clarify for students that not all connections to the text are connections based on inferential thinking. The second aspect of inferring is similar to a weaving process in which the reader follows the different strands of the story that the author has created to give meaning to the text. In the course of trying to gain insight and interpret the intent of each strand as they try to weave them together, readers develop dynamic relationships with the text. Therefore, our second goal was to show students how to develop these relationships.

Using the Arts to Teach Inferring

Art invites viewers in, as they try to interpret meaning by interlacing their own schema with that of the artist. The arts offer an immediate entry into inferential thinking, thus enabling our students to have experiences with this strategy quickly. Using the arts also allowed us to create numerous opportunities for students to encounter the need to infer; therefore, students quickly developed fluency with this strategy. One day we had students listen to a piece of music to interpret its meaning, and the next day we had them interview a character from a book to discover the character's inner thoughts and feelings. In both cases, the students expanded on and applied their inferential thinking. We found that the multidimensional aspect of using an artistic approach exposed them to a variety of experiences that allowed all students to use inferential thinking. Through this multifaceted understanding of inferring, students were able to use this strategy more effectively with text.

An In-Depth Look at Teaching Inferring Through a Study of Matisse

When thinking about how to teach inferring to the second-grade class, we decided to use an artist study of Henri Matisse. We bought a Matisse calendar and borrowed a few prints from another teacher. The first day, Sabine read *Matisse: An Introduction to the Artist's Life and Work*, by Antony Mason (1995). This book emphasizes the significant stylistic changes that occurred to Matisse as an artist. That is, it shows how Matisse changed from being a realistic painter to being part of the fauve movement in painting (a French expressionist movement), and finally, to being a collage artist. We specifically chose to study Matisse because he was curious about how color and shape influenced the viewer's interaction with the picture. The students were fascinated when they learned that he would spend months looking at the way a picture's "feeling" would change when he changed the background color.

When we met again the next morning, the children gathered on the rug. On the blackboard, we had hung a poster with different colored construction paper on the top. We began by initially placing a simple white Matisse-style leaf on the green construction paper and asking students to think about what feeling the color expressed. Once the students had shared their thinking, we moved on to the next color and continued until we had covered each color on the poster. The chart in Figure 16 shows the students' thinking during this color-exploration activity.

At the end of this activity, it was apparent that the students were struck by how much the background color really changed the way they perceived a picture. Next, the students listened to a reading and explored the contents of *Matisse: Art Activity Pack* (Boutan, 1996) and viewed Matisse's *Creole Dancer*. The book shows how this picture looks with a black background, as well as a multicolored background. At this point, the students interjected that they thought Matisse had made the right choice using a multicolored background because it made the painting more "alive." Specifically, one student pointed out that because the picture is about a dancer, the colored paper gave the impression of movement. There were a few children, however, who liked the black background because they felt it made the picture itself stand out more. The students were beginning to use their inferential thinking to follow Matisse's clue; that is, by changing the color, he was able to guide their feelings about the picture, even though that feeling might not be explicit.

To further deepen the students' understanding of the power of color, we had them experiment with creating simple collages. Our intent was to see if students could try to develop a feeling, as well as an image, in their art. We gave each student a black, a white, and a multicolored piece of paper to use

Figure 16   Chart Showing Students' Thoughts During a Color-Exploration Activity

Yellow	Green	Red	Blue	Black
excited	puzzled	burning	misty	sly
happy	lonely	challenged	free	small
joyful	curious	mad	calm	serious
active	mysterious	hungry	sleepy	magical
burning	powerful	furious	mysterious	lonely
fiery	peaceful	active	frustrated	scary

for the collage's background. Colored construction paper was also available to them on the table in the back of the room. Matisse prints decorated the walls of the classroom and surrounded the students as they worked on simple, nondetailed shapes for their collages. They made the same shape for all three backgrounds. Then, students spent time thinking about how each collage made them feel. As the students completed their collages, we asked them to write down the feeling they associated with each picture. Figure 17 shows each of Sierra's collages. About the collages, Sierra wrote,

> I think the colored one is the best because they are the colors of nature and they make me feel excited. I want the person looking at it to feel happy.

Through engaging in the creative process of collage making, students learned to see beyond form to the more emotive aspects of the artwork. Students' thinking about their pieces of art was similar to the thinking in which competent readers engage as they make inferences about a piece of writing.

To observe students' ability to use this strategy, we asked them to make another Matisse-style collage and to write a poem about it. We wanted to assess whether students could use shape and color to affect the emotive quality of their work. Each student started by designing a picture, then worked on changing each shape in the picture into something more simple and symbolic. Once students had the overall image in mind, a great deal of their

Figure 17   Sierra's Color Collages

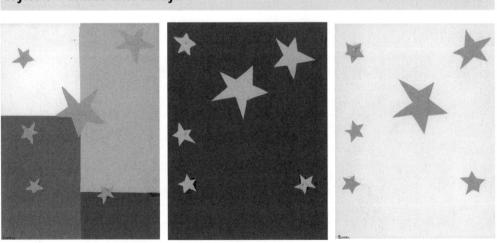

time went into choosing the perfect color background and arranging the shapes. After finishing their collages, students inferred the emotional qualities of the collages and wrote them in poems. One student, Emily, spent a great deal of time on her project, even asking to stay in at recess in order to complete her poem. Figure 18 shows Emily's collage and poem; her poem demonstrates the emotions that the collage evoked for her.

After observing students as they worked on the project and viewing the end result, we believed they understood that pieces of art could be about not only the objects in the image but also the emotions the artist wants the work to evoke. The arts enabled the students to learn about inferring in more than one context, which helped them build a mental model of the strategy that was more complex than if they had only been exposed to inferring using text. This model became the basis these students could draw from when they inferred while reading. Three weeks after we had finished our study on inferring and Matisse, Ella came shyly into the classroom on the arm of her father. She quickly pulled out a folded piece of newspaper and related how she had found this piece when her father had been reading the Sunday paper. She told Sabine, "Look, there's a Matisse. It says that Matisse's art is coming to Denver.

Figure 18   Emily's Collage and Poem

Blue

Blue tastes like foam shimmering on water

Blue smells like a dream come true

Blue looks like velvet in the sun

Blue sounds like clouds whispering

Blue feels like a thick sky

Blue

Can I share this with the class?" Ella's father told me how excited she had been to be able to recognize an artist in the paper. This was the beginning of a new type of reading for Ella. She started to skim newspapers and magazines to find articles to show the class. Ella never read the whole article, but she used what she learned about inferring to highlight what the text was about and how that related to what we were studying. From then on, she became our designated class researcher.

Art-Based Lessons for Teaching Inferring

Using Poetry to Develop Emotional Inferential Thinking

Grades: 1–5

Text Resources: poems with emotive qualities, such as "Tree Horse" (George, 1998a), "Poem," (Hughes, 1994b), and "Poor" (Johnston, 1996)

Lesson: Poetry seemed like a natural way to bridge the arts and inferential thinking. We wanted to use poetry because it is often open-ended, and although it guides the reader in a direction, it requires him or her to interpret to gain meaning. Ultimately, it is the reader's responsibility to infer deeper meaning from the piece. Poetry encourages the reader to draw conclusions based on an intermingling of the reader's understanding of the world with what the poet has written.

We began this lesson with second graders using Hughes's poem, which was written on the board. This simple, short poem depicts the feelings a person has when a friend leaves. We had chosen this poem because it was emotionally powerful and built on an experience that all the children had encountered. Also, the language Hughes uses was accessible to every child.

After listening to a read-aloud of the poem, each student read it silently. When students finished reading, we posed specific questions focusing on the underlying emotions of the piece to help encourage inferential thinking. Instead of asking what the poem was about, we asked, "What feelings do you have when you read the poem?" This question elicited a barrage of comments: "being alone," "being left out," "isolation," "feeling sad, unhappy, even a little scared." As a group, we then discussed which parts of the poem gave students the strongest feelings and what those feelings were. Many students quickly said that the lines "he went away from me / there's nothing more to say" (p. 12) were the most powerful of the poem. One student, Matthew, told us that in these lines, the author was showing how people can feel left out and alone when others leave them. In the past, we might have had a few of these types of comments, but we also would have had generalized comments that it was about a child who leaves or about someone who loses a friend. It was apparent from this discussion that all the students had made the leap from seeing the literal aspects in the poem to inferring the poem's tone.

We then moved to another poem, "Tree Horse" (George, 1998a), about a child who pretends his tree is a horse that he is riding. We chose to use this poem because its emotive qualities contrast to those in Hughes's poem and because it is a more difficult poem. The poem was written on a large piece of paper attached to the chalkboard, but each student also had an individual copy. Again, the students listened to a read-aloud of this poem, then read it silently.

After they finished reading, the students wrote down their thoughts. Their responses to the poem varied, as they noted it had the feelings of freedom and of being "happy," "afraid," "strong and fast," "excited," "crazy," "powerful," and "frightened." Their responses were focused on certain lines, such as "we leap into the wind" and "plunges his head down" (p. 21), but also showed how inferring involves a uniquely personalized process. For some students the poem conjured up feelings of fright, whereas for other students it conjured feelings of excitement. By weaving the poet's meaning with their own personal responses, students clearly were in the process of using inferential thought.

For the final poem, we chose Tony Johnston's "Poor"—which depicts a scarecrow in the November cold—and decided to have the students work independently by reading it silently. By this point, the students felt comfortable with the lesson and after they finished reading, went right to work writing down their thoughts. Again, there was a wide range of responses— "frightened," "scared," "cold," "hungry," "dying," "worried," "lonely"—but all the students seemed to find the underlying tone of the poem.

Reflection: For the students, poetry turned out to be a gentle entry point into inferring from text. Poems often rely on only a few words to paint a picture and show a feeling. They also require the readers to bring their own thoughts and understandings of the world to the reading in order to infer the meaning of the whole piece. Using poetry enabled the students to incorporate two main aspects of inferring: using prior knowledge and interpreting the author's intent within the text.

Using Music to Generate Inferential Thinking

Grades: 1–3

Materials: a mix of instruments and other objects used to make rhythms

Text Resource: *Frog Odyssey* (Snape & Snape, 1991)

Lesson: We used this lesson when the first-grade class was doing a nature study. We began with a read-aloud of *Frog Odyssey*, a book about frogs that must leave their trash-filled pond because builders start filling in the pond. Their journey to find a new home takes the frogs through different dangerous situations. After reading the book to the children, we placed drums, chimes, sticks, and bells in front of them. Our goal was to have the students listen to the book again and then create a musical journey that matched the frogs' journey. We hoped the students would infer what types of sounds would match the actions and emotions of different parts of the journey.

After the students took their instruments, we let them have a few minutes to experiment with the types of sounds the instruments could make. But to help keep students focused on the book and the directions we had given them, we asked them to place the instruments behind them while the book was read again.

During the second reading of the book, Sabine stopped at different parts to discuss and decide what type of instrument would make the right sound to illustrate that part of the story. For example, for when the frogs find out they must leave their home, the students chose a slow, deep drumbeat to reflect the seriousness of the scene. But for later in the story, when the frogs encounter the cat, students wanted to use bells and shakers to make the music livelier. The thoughtful and lively discussion that took place while we tried to determine what instruments to use led to the students' strong comprehension of the text. Once we had decided on music for the whole story, the book was read for a third time with the musical accompaniment.

Reflection: Throughout this lesson, the students consistently had to use their prior knowledge about sounds and the effects of those sounds in order to re-create the frogs' journey. As previously noted, using prior knowledge is a significant aspect of inferential thinking. This lesson also helped focus the students on the story elements that seemed most critical. At points, they had to move beyond what was stated explicitly by the author and construe their own personal meanings. Using music encouraged students to dive into the text deeper to infer meaning that would help them produce the appropriate piece of music.

You can also do the same lesson with your students using books with more complex themes such as *How Many Days to America: A Thanksgiving Story* (Bunting, 1990). This book, about a group of refugees' struggle to reach the United States in a small boat, also would work well for this lesson because the plot centers on a journey.

Using Famous Paintings to Develop Inferring

Grades: 3–5

Text Resource: *The Witch of Blackbird Pond* (Speare, 1958)

Art Resources: American colonial and Caribbean artwork (calendars also work well)

Lesson: As part of a study of colonial America, we separated fifth-grade students into small groups. One group read *The Witch of Blackbird Pond*. The main character in this book, a young woman named Kit, is forced to move from Barbados to New England. The main internal struggle for Kit is reconciling her laidback island lifestyle with the more rigid requirements of life in New England. When the students in this group began discussing and making inferences about Kit, their comments were relatively superficial. To help the students in their thinking, we bought a calendar of Caribbean artwork and one of colonial artwork to share with them. The first picture we shared with students from the Caribbean calendar was colorful and free flowing, similar to Kit's memories of Barbados. The next picture we presented depicted colonial women sitting in a circle and quilting. Everything about the picture was controlled—the colors, the painting style, and even the women themselves. After examining the two paintings, the students were able to infer much more about Kit's internal struggle, as evidenced by their profound thoughts and comments. Rachel, for example, noticed the extreme difference in the artwork and in the cultures and said, "Look at all the color and light in the Caribbean picture. It looks so free. But the other one is so strict looking."

We then asked this group to create a picture representing its insights about Kit. The group produced a beautiful painting of a Connecticut saltbox house (a particular shape of house from colonial New England), with large windows from which rich red curtains billowed. When the students explained their painting of the house, they talked about how, outside her house, Kit keeps up all the formal requirements that New England life requires. Inside her house, however, Kit can be more free and colorful, representing her

Barbadian heritage. The students also noted that the red curtains would let the New Englanders know that Kit is different.

Reflection: By looking at two prints, students were able to compare different places and cultures. These visual images highlighted for students how difficult it might be to have to switch homelands. By developing the students' imagery around the topic through the use of prints, we then were able to help students gain prior knowledge that led them to make richer inferences about the text.

Using Process Drama as a Pathway to Inferring

Grades: 2–4

Text Resource: *Roberto Clemente* (Gresko, 1997)

Lesson: A group of second-grade students read the biography *Roberto Clemente* as part of a book club. During their reading, the students focused on using the three comprehension strategies that we already had explored with them: (1) building and activating schema, (2) questioning, and (3) inferring. When we first discussed this book with them, most students' comments revolved around making a connection to events in their own lives or asking a question, but few went deeper into the text and Clemente's life. Therefore, we decided to use process drama to increase the students' thinking, because it is a short activity and it worked well with the hardships described in Clemente's biography (see Appendix B for more on process drama).

We wrote down six characters—Clemente, three white people unhappy to be around Puerto Ricans, and two other people in the park depicted in a scene from the book—on small pieces of paper and placed the papers in a hat. After students picked their parts, we presented each of them with a scenario. We presented each student with details only about what his or her character was going to do and gave all of them a few minutes to think about these instructions. The scene would begin with all the characters meeting in the park.

Once the scene started, we gave the students no direction unless it helped them to stay in their roles. At first, it was hard for students who played the characters who asked Clemente to leave the park to express anger or have a negative attitude toward a fellow classmate, but eventually, they were able to get into the role. The boy playing Clemente was clearly uncomfortable with his situation: He did not want to provoke more anger or leave the park. The two students playing the other people sitting in the park sat silently, unable to move or take any action. This scene lasted about three minutes. When it was over, the students quickly started talking. The boy who played Clemente said, "I can't believe what a strong person Roberto must have been. He was able to stay calm and not show anger to people who were being awful to him."

Reflection: This short but powerful drama helped all the students understand Clemente's life story in a new, more powerful way. The students had to grapple with the emotions that accompanied the situations presented in the drama. They were not given scripts and did not know how Clemente would react to the situation. Thus, they had to infer from what they already knew about Clemente and make their own decisions about how he and the other characters would act. This type of thinking helped the students comprehend the more significant aspects of Clemente's biography. We observed that when they returned to their discussion of the book, students made more thoughtful comments about who Clemente was and the difficult situations he encountered.

Using a Study of Ancient Art to Teach Inferring

Grades: 3–5

Text Resource: *Ancient Egypt* (Morris, 2000), or other books that show pictures of art from an ancient culture

Lesson: Similar to the work of archeologists, the third graders' study of ancient Egypt heavily relied on looking at artwork and artifacts from the culture to gain meaning. Through this process, students were able to make insightful inferences about what ancient Egypt really was like. To teach inferring to the third graders, we decided to elaborate on this process by using a concrete study of ancient Egyptian art.

To prepare, we searched through all the books we had about ancient Egypt. One book we discovered was titled *Ancient Egypt*. This book, organized into categories such as daily life, entertainment, and writing and literature, became the basis for our lesson because of its reproductions of ancient Egyptian art. In each of the categories, the author uses a piece of art to explore that area of Egyptian life. Besides just showing the piece of art, the book also gives a detailed account of what symbols in the art represent.

We began the lesson by showing the class a picture of ancient Egyptian gods and goddesses and asking students to think about what this picture told them about Egyptian life. Because we covered the words on the page, the students' inferences had to be their own. Sabine listed their responses and asked students to refer to the picture to help support their inferences.

Children made a variety of assessments such as "Egyptian [people] really loved birds," "They wore a lot of jewelry," and "They liked to wear costumes." After all the students had shared their thoughts, Roberta read the beginning of the section that states the picture is about gods and goddesses. We then asked the class to return to their inferences about the picture and see if this new information changed their thinking. Some students now thought that maybe Egyptians worshiped birds because a person in the picture appears to be handing two small jars to a bird-like creature. However, it was apparent that some students were making comments that were true but not based on information from the picture. So as students continued to share, we kept reminding them to support their inferences with clues from the picture. Also, we made sure to draw parallels between the strategies the students were using with the strategies they could use while reading.

Next, we divided students into small groups and gave each group photocopied pictures of other pieces of ancient Egyptian art. Using aspects of the pictures to support and prove its inferences, each group had to make a list similar to the one we had created as a class. The groups had 15 minutes to work before they came back as a whole class to share their work.

Reflection: Throughout this final activity, the students continued to use inferring to learn about ancient Egyptian culture. Many groups had lively debates about what an artifact was or what it might symbolize. One group had a difficult time coming up with one group interpretation about a picture, so they decided to share all the students' different ideas about what the picture represented. Through the arts, the class became aware of how important it is to look carefully at artwork in order to make rich, meaningful inferences about the artist's intent. While reading, students used the text to determine the author's intent and their prior knowledge to make inferences about the text as a whole. This lesson successfully taught students how to use inferring to help gain comprehension of a particular topic.

Using an Image Mosaic to Adapt Inferences

Grades: K–5

Materials: posters of animals or portraits of famous people, chart paper, black felt-tip pens

Lesson: One concept of inferring that is often elusive to children is learning how to revise their thinking while reading. Although they make reasonable predictions based on their inferences, children often do not revise these predictions as a story develops. We thought that by manipulating images using an image mosaic, we would be able to highlight this process for students, thus making it easier for them to transfer this strategy to reading. We worked first with a kindergarten class and then a fourth-grade class, changing the lesson only a little to meet the differing needs of the individual students.

For the kindergarten class, we had chosen to use a large poster of a bear. The class was about to begin a bear study, and this activity was going to be one part of their introduction to the study. We pinned the picture to the bulletin board and covered it with a piece of chart paper. On the chart paper, we had drawn large puzzle pieces (enough for each student in the class to cut out one piece).

The students sat on the floor, wondering aloud what was behind the puzzle. We explained to them that they would take turns cutting out puzzle pieces and then making predictions about what the picture behind the puzzle might be. One by one, students came up and cut a piece, and as they did, Roberta listed what students thought the image might be. Students supported their ideas by pointing to aspects of the pictures on the back of their puzzle pieces. After the first two pieces had been removed, most of the children were sure the picture was of a dog because of the brown fur. But after the third piece was cut, they suddenly saw a claw. The students then started a whole new list of which animals it might be. At that point, we focused the conversation on why the students' revised their thinking. After the whole picture was revealed to the students, we discussed how good readers also revise their thinking when they read.

Because the kindergartners loved this lesson, we decided to start studies with other classes in the same manner. The fourth-grade class had been studying famous explorers, and we wanted to help students learn how to adapt their inferences as they learned more about the explorer they were studying. For this project, we used a small black-and-white portrait of Captain James Cook.

We led the fourth graders through a similar discussion but used a different type of imaging technique. We made a grid over the portrait using 1-inch squares. On the back of each square, we placed a different number. Then, we cut up the pieces and placed them in a basket. We passed out one 10-inch square to each student as we explained the directions for this lesson. Each student then picked out one of the small squares from the basket and used a black felt-tip pen to copy the image from the small square to the big square. To make the process easier for the students, we showed them techniques to make this transfer, such as telling them to look at one side of the small square or explaining that if a line started in the middle of the small square, students should start a similar line in the middle of the larger square. We made sure to have many extra 10-inch squares so frustrated students could start again.

Some students' squares were more complicated, so students who finished quickly picked a second square to copy. Once all the squares were complete, it was time to build the image. We began with number one in the upper-left corner and slowly built across and then down. Similar to the kindergartners, the fourth graders went piece by piece, making predictions about what the completed image might be and changing their predictions as more pieces were in place.

Reflection: In each of these lessons, students built an image one piece at a time. When students saw only a small piece of the image, they naturally used their spatial reasoning skills to determine what the whole image would be. The ongoing process of building an image mosaic gave students the opportunity to use metacognitive strategies to explore how their inferences developed with each new piece of information. In our discussions, we linked the students' abilities in these lessons to what good readers do while they read—revise inferential thoughts as they gain information.

Final Thoughts

This chapter demonstrated how the arts open new doors to help students learn complex strategies that will help them comprehend text. Inferring is a difficult strategy for students to become comfortable using while reading; often they are looking for an exact answer within the text. By using different forms of communication such as drawing or music that require the students to infer meaning, we were able to help students develop their use of inferential thinking. We were only able to help students transfer their learning of this strategy to text because they understood the strategy of inferring and had become comfortable using it. The variety of experiences that students had using the strategy helped them become comfortable using it and led to their success at using inferring while reading.

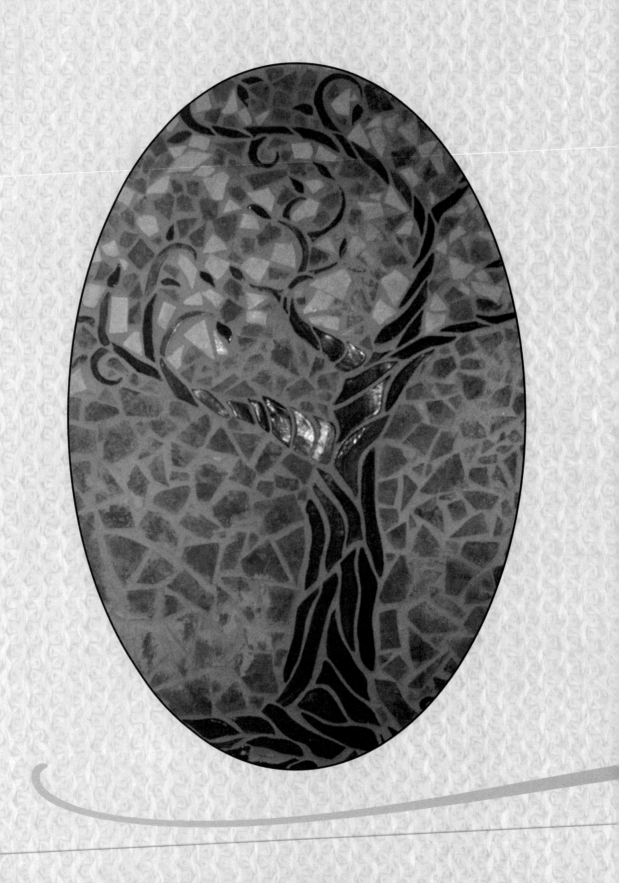

Chapter 7

Synthesis

It is not so often the case that
we can learn in the presence of
compelling objects that engage our
senses, allow for many kinds of
cognition, connect to many facets
of life, sustain our attention, and
so on. Art is an opportunity. Let us
not miss it.

—David Perkins, 1994, p. 5

Inside the doorway of our school stands a grand mosaic of a tree. The third graders created this 5-foot mosaic with Roberta and a visiting artist. Sitting at a long table with thousands of small pieces of colored ceramics, the students easily could have been overwhelmed, but they launched into this project with their usual enthusiasm. They needed a great deal of focus, collaborative effort on the part of each student, and the ability to build thousands of small pieces into their vision of a tree.

Faced with those glittery pieces in front of us that would become the tree mosaic, we muse over this process and how it is similar to our thinking about synthesis. We are asking children to align their images with one another and the vision of the final mosaic. In order to help them develop the strategy of synthesis while reading, we guide students in blending their images, connections, prior knowledge, and inferences with the author's intent to build meaning. We want children to rely on their personal interpretations of text within a structure that adds clarity and new understandings of the text. However, we do not want children reading fiction or nonfiction and arriving at a new synthesis that leads to a misunderstanding of the topic.

What Is Synthesis?

Keene and Zimmermann (1997) describe synthesis as "organizing the different pieces to create a mosaic, a meaning, a beauty, greater than the sum of each shiny piece" (p. 169). Synthesis is a combination of retelling and organizing that creates a summary of the text. As they read, readers often use this process to scaffold their understanding of a text. In other words, readers internally organize their ideas and develop new meanings. To help children develop this ability, we structured the reading of a text so that there were natural breaks. During these breaks, we used the arts to strengthen the retelling and organizational skills children needed to synthesize text.

Using the Arts to Teach Synthesis

At its best, synthesis helps readers generate new ideas. Readers move beyond the process of weaving the author's thoughts with their own experiences and create new meanings. Take, for example, a fourth-grade construction project in which we challenged students to build the tallest structure they could using 30 straws. Most groups started by building a tree-like structure, taping straws one on top of another and using three straws as base-like roots, which had little or no success. Meanwhile, one group chose a cube structure that produced a stable base allowing that group to build higher. As other groups watched, they began to use this successful cube structure also. However, each group that incorporated this structure added a unique twist. One group, for example, chose to build a rectangular shape using fewer straws, which allowed that group to build an even taller structure. Another group integrated the cube structure with a pyramid shape, and it was this group that created the tallest structure. During this project, we observed children using synthesis as they altered a successful building strategy to develop their own personal approaches.

We have found that students deepen their ability to synthesize ideas and information when they are given a variety of arts approaches. Working with and studying the arts help children experience different styles of art, which they then blend with their own technique and vision to create original pieces of art. Synthesizing text involves the same process, enabling students to comprehend the author's message and blend it with their own thoughts and ideas to create deeper meaning.

An In-Depth Look at Teaching Synthesis Through the Dramatic Interview

The arts give children a concrete framework in which to develop synthesis, specifically helping them to retell and organize. The arts give students the images and metaphors from which new ideas arise. We used the dramatic interview (see Appendix B for specifics on this drama technique) to encourage children's synthesis of the meaning of a text. When Jan's fourth graders were producing a play of *William Shakespeare's* A Midsummer Night's Dream (Coville, 1996), she expressed concern to us that they were missing some of its significant themes. We, therefore, decided that the children should engage in a dramatic interview to explore the struggle between Oberon and Titania, king and queen of the fairies, over the human child. As Betty Jane Wagner (1998) states, "The goal of educational drama is to create an experience through which students may come to understand human interactions, empathize with other people, and internalize alternative points of view" (p. 5). Because the dramatic interview gives participants the chance to improvise dialogue, we believed it would lead students to think more deeply about the themes of the play while making personal connections.

During one of the students' rehearsals, we began by asking the students playing Oberon and Titania to stop and allow other students to ask them questions. First, we gave each student a copy of a portion of the dialogue in the scene. Then, we asked the students to highlight text that puzzled them and write down their questions in a double-entry journal format, placing the text on one side and leaving room for comments on the other side. If they could follow up their questions with inferences of their own, they also could write those on one side of the journal. We knew from experience that this process would help students focus on the play and their questions about it.

After students wrote down their questions, they began posing these to the characters of Oberon and Titania during the interview. As they tried to answer students' questions, we could see the students playing Oberon and Titania trying to comprehend the struggle they were acting out in the play. With each question, students gradually brought their own experiences to the discussion, which allowed them to use prior knowledge, inferential thinking, authentic questioning, and synthesis to produce a more complex understanding of the play. The questions in the following dialogue show the students' range of thinking:

Annie: Why do you want the boy so much?

Titania: I promised his mother that I would take care of him, and she was my friend.

Oberon: Puck isn't smart enough to help me. I need the boy.

Steven: Are you jealous of each other?

Titania: He shouldn't have everything he wants.

Oberon: Titania is always complaining.

Ben: What does the boy want?

Oberon: It doesn't matter what he wants because I need him.

Jassie: Why don't you two just live together and share the boy?

Oberon: Titania is too angry.

We found that when using the arts in this way, students were challenged in their ability to think critically and synthesize, often arriving at an *aha* moment. Wagner (1998) explains, "Participants are testing hypotheses, inviting supposition, and experiencing the art of logical argument. As participants experience the perspectives of various roles, they not only see the world from other viewpoints but they also enlarge their understandings" (p. 9). When this happened in Jan's class, students often exclaimed, "Oh, now I get it!" The arts gave them new confidence in their own ability to interact with demanding text.

Before the dramatic interview, we recorded students' reflections concerning the struggle between Oberon and Titania by asking them, "Describe how Oberon and Titania's relationship affects the play?" We asked students the same question after the interview to assess how the dramatic interview helped develop their thinking. See Figure 19 for Amalia's responses. Her response after the interview clearly shows the growth in her critical thinking about one of the more complex themes of the play.

Figure 19   Amalia's Responses Before and After the Dramatic Interview

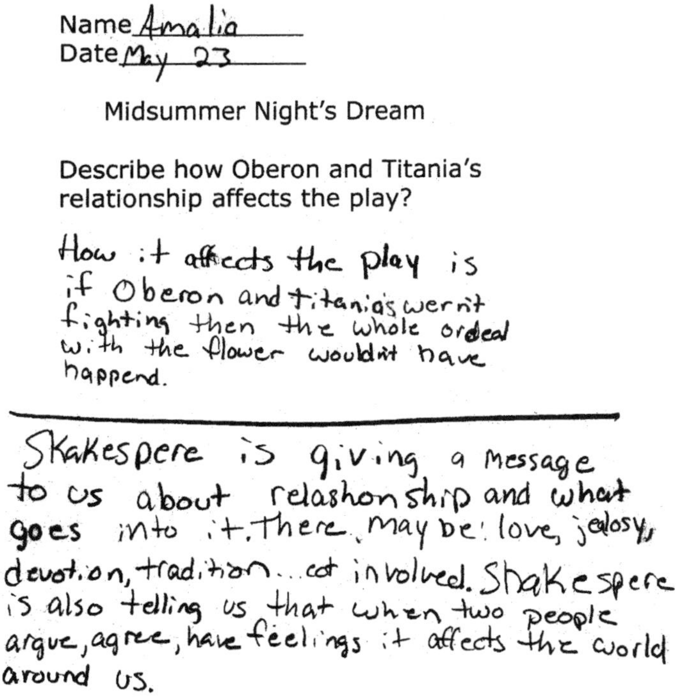

Name Amalia
Date May 23

Midsummer Night's Dream

Describe how Oberon and Titania's
relationship affects the play?

How it affects the play is
if Oberon and titanias wern't
fighting then the whole ordeal
with the flower wouldn't have
happend.

Skakespere is giving a message
to us about relashonship and what
goes into it. There may be love, jealosy,
devotion, tradition...ect involved. Shakespere
is also telling us that when two people
argue, agree, have feelings it affects the world
around us.

During the interview, we also charted students' questions and answers; afterward, we helped them label their questions and answers to show them when they were using inferences and their prior knowledge to understand the characters' struggle. Some students were able to connect Oberon and Titania's struggle to the one their own parents had encountered during divorce. These students spoke eloquently about the feelings they had when angry adults made them feel stuck in the middle of these struggles. It also was apparent from the change we saw in children's answers to our question that the dramatic interview had sparked their ability to synthesize ideas and come to a better understanding of characters and their motives. During this activity, it was important to chart the growth of students' thinking so that they—not just us—could see how questioning, inferring, prior knowledge, and imagery worked together to build synthesis.

Art-Based Lessons for Teaching Synthesis

Using Dramatic Interviews With Young Children to Distill Important Ideas From a Fairy Tale

Grades: 1–2

Text Resource: *Wishbones: A Folk Tale From China* (Wilson, 1993)

Lesson: We were working with groups of first and second graders involved in a study of Cinderella variations. Although the well-known versions in the United States were widely accepted and understood by these children, versions from other countries were not as accessible for them. Early in the study, we chose to read a Chinese variation titled *Wishbones*. This version is different enough that children often do not recognize it as a Cinderella story until they hear about the lost slipper. The story is reserved in its storytelling approach, so there are wonderful places to stop and invite children to take on the role of a character for a dramatic interview in order to interpret the story more fully (again, see Appendix B for specifics on the dramatic interview). We used a piece of silk as a costume and tied it in different ways so children would have a moment to transition into their characters. As they took turns sitting in a special chair reserved for the character being interviewed, children accepted questions from the class about the story.

Our first interviewee was the main character of *Wishbones*, Yeh Hsien, who has lost her mother and lives with her stepmother and stepsister. Children asked her how she felt about having to work so hard, and they wanted to know why her father does not support her. In general, students' questions varied and required both concrete and in-depth answers. With some groups of children, we needed to model throughout the interview the kinds of questions that helped to better understand the story, whereas other groups seemed to know quickly how to ask questions that centered on the meaning of the story.

The next character interviewed was the fish. Initial questions about the color, scent, and feel of the fish showed us how visual the children were as they began to construct their mental models of the story. As we moved through the story and the characters, however, children became experts at asking questions and discovering more about the meaning of the story. They began to explore characters' feelings and motives, as well as significant events. By the end of the interviews, each child was clinging to his or her role and asking questions as his or her character. This unexpected result of the dramatic interviews added another dimension to the students' dialogue. After we finished the story, we talked with children about the ways their questions, inferences, and images may have contributed to their synthesis of the story's meaning.

Reflection: Using dramatic interviews in a study of comparative texts enabled children to search for important ideas common to similar stories from different cultures. The interactive nature of the interview involved children in the story as participants, not observers or listeners. For children who were primarily kinesthetic learners, it not only gave them the opportunity to use their bodies as they mimicked characters, but also assisted them in thinking about the meaning of the story. After interviewing each character, children seemed more at ease synthesizing the significance of each character into their overall understanding of the story and its meaning. Children made more connections between characters and evolved in their understanding of the relationships that made the story whole.

Using Poetry to Increase the Quality of Attention

Grades: 3–5

Text Resources: *Out of the Dust* (Hesse, 1997), *Children of the Dust Bowl: The True Story of the School at Weedpatch Camp* (Stanley, 1992), and a collection of poems such as *What Have You Lost?* (Nye, 1999)

Lesson: Our fifth-grade book club began in September and met throughout the year. We had a core group of three girls, who were gifted in the literary arts. Through the year, other students interested in the then-current book choice joined us. We selected books primarily for their strong characters because we wanted to have book discussions that helped prepare the students for their transition to middle school.

During one meeting of our book club in which we were reading *Out of the Dust* came frank discussions of the girls' own personal struggles. The narrator of this book, 12-year-old Billie Joe, shares honest, moving descriptions of her life and losses during the Dust Bowl days of the 1930s in Oklahoma, USA. Through the discussion, it became apparent that these girls had losses, too: Daniella was struggling to cope with the loss of her father, Samantha was angry about a recent family move that uprooted her from her friends, and Maya was upset about the attention her parents gave to a sibling with a chronic illness. The girls listened intently to one another with compassion and support. Because they identified with Billie Joe, they easily understood why she feels alone and frightened and needs adult support.

Our goal with all students throughout our work with the arts was to show them a variety of ways to concentrate on gaining deeper comprehension of text. Focus is an important skill for both novice and expert readers, as even expert readers still need to increase the quality of their attention to their reading. We tried to instill this skill in each student as we taught these strategies, and we discovered that we sometimes needed to teach focus in a multitude of ways. After their discussion about the book and their own lives, we asked the girls to focus on the book and offer a list of words related to its important images. Roberta recorded these words on a chart:

Image	Word
dust	dryness
hopes buried	horror
motherless child	piano

Next, we read poems from Naomi Shihab Nye's collection *What Have You Lost?* (1999), such as "Invisibility." Immersing students in poetry was part of what Susan Wooldridge, in *Poemcrazy: Freeing Your Life With Words* (1996), calls "setting up circumstances in which poems are likely to happen" (p. xii). We chose to use "Invisibility" because it seems to express a feeling that children may have in school when classrooms get crowded or at home when parents get busy. Nye's collection of poems highlights for children how other people have faced losses and how some of these people have grown stronger because of these losses.

To experience what life was like during the Dust Bowl, we also listened to ragtime piano music; drank homemade lemonade, as if assuaging a dusty thirst; and read firsthand accounts of life during this time from Jerry Stanley's *Children of the Dust Bowl: The True Story of the School at Weedpatch Camp.* We immersed ourselves in the language of Hesse's book, in her rich descriptions of the prairie and the characters' lives. The resources we provided and the class discussion helped the girls delve into their own lives, making connections and inferences as they shared about the text.

Finally, the girls wrote reflection poems tying together their understanding of the book, its characters, and their own lives (see Maya's poem in Figure 20). The girls used poetry to summarize their thoughts about the struggles Billie Joe faces, as well as their own struggles.

Figure 20   Maya's Reflection Poem

Dust

A world of dust
Dust on the houses
Dust in the fields
A blizzard of dust is all I can
See
Then... when it clears
father... only dimly aware of
me, of my life.

Digging his pond
Digging his grave
Hopes buried in Dust
I am running away from
myself
finding only me
but I won't give up

Reflection: Writing poetry gave our students space to form a cohesive thought, memory, hope, or another way of presenting a summary or synthesis with meaning and beauty. Poetry was a format that encouraged the girls to choose precise, meaningful words to express their thoughts. This format also gave them an opportunity to create a focused summary of important points of the text and an avenue for relating these points to their own experiences. According to Wooldridge (1996), "Poems go to the essence of things from the inside out. What science tends to take apart, poetry senses and takes in whole" (p. 106). For these students who were intrapersonal learners, whose strength was having a heightened awareness of their own feelings, poetry was a way to synthesize those feelings with the text.

Using Process Drama for a Collaborative Construction of Meaning

Grades: 4–5

Materials: optional props such as capes, wax and an insignia, and parchment paper

Text Resources: *Anna of Byzantium* (Barrett, 1999) and *Catherine, Called Birdy* (Cushman, 1994)

Lesson: The purple and gold cover of *Anna of Byzantium* made students in the fifth-grade book club feel like they could hold the book close, take it home, and crawl into a big, comfortable chair with it. Perhaps the study of medieval history the year before—which included a reading of *Catherine, Called Birdy*, a book the students loved—properly prepared the students for *Anna of Byzantium*.

The story of Anna is one that brings readers through a maze of feelings, in which trust is built, dismantled, and then rebuilt as they come to know the characters more deeply. The girls in our book club (Daniella, Maya, and Samantha) easily shared connections to the text, made predictions and inferences, and asked questions. But there were still important layers and themes in the text that they had yet to discover. Daniella, in particular, related so much of her own struggle with the loss of her father to the character of Anna that we feared she would begin to miss who the real Anna is. So we introduced process drama (for more on this technique, refer to Appendix B). Process drama is not meant to create a performance for an audience, as the process itself is the purpose. The goal is to have the students enter into the emotions and thinking of the characters they portray. As previously discussed, children enter into the lives and viewpoints of the characters, then create their own action and dialogue around the dilemma the teacher presents. The process helps students not only understand the characters' viewpoints and the author's intent, but also moves them to explore their own ideas as well as those of their peers.

We began by asking students to come to this book club prepared to participate in a short drama. When they entered the room, they chose slips of paper on a table, which indicated the characters they would be. Students then put on silk capes in the form of a royal gown or a servant's apron—whatever best signified a change of roles for them. The letter introducing the scene was delivered once the students were ready. We had chosen to write a letter to Anna from her sister, Maria, after Anna is banished to a convent in the mountains. This letter explained one of the book's dilemmas; therefore, it invited responses from all the characters and posed a problem that they would need to solve with thoughtfulness, as there were a variety of ramifications. We wrote the following letter on parchment paper and sealed it with a wax insignia:

> Dearest Anna,
>
> I am writing to you, dear sister, in hopes that this letter finds you in good health. Our brother, Emperor John, has asked me to write to you. We heard that your books about Father were finished, and we send you our congratulations. We are hoping that you might come for a visit and bring the books with you. We are in danger of being taken over by the Turks, and John thinks that perhaps Father's story might yield the secret of what he should do next. I believe John might reward you by giving you that small cottage near the forest. I would love to have you back, dear sister. Please consider this matter.
>
> With all my love, Maria

The dialogue that emerged as a result of this letter and the letter that the girls wrote in response showed how the collaborative process moved them in their thinking until it seemed that they discovered a great deal more about the characters, as well as themselves. The process imposed a structure that helped them to think more deeply about the text and synthesize diverse perspectives into a cohesive whole.

During the drama, we participated by taking on roles with the students and were able to return them to the authority of the text gently with our questions. Students challenged one another as they debated their response to the letter. Girls who initially responded with their own emotions by threatening to kill Emperor John were brought back to the author's intent and gradually were able to synthesize who the characters were in order to predict what their behaviors might be outside the story. Their letter of response showed their growing understanding of the author's purpose:

Dearest Maria,

I would be quite happy to send the books to John for him to read if he *can* read! However, I am quite happy here with the sisters at the convent and wish to remain. I am quite concerned about Mother's health and only wish that brother John would release her to come and stay with me here.

Your sister,
Anna

After finishing our drama, we asked the girls to write about how Anna had changed in relation to issues of power. Simone wrote,

I think that Anna's sense of power over people or a place, but she wanted power over herself and her felings [*sic*]. She no longer wanted a servant but a friend. Her hunger was no longer for power, but for friendship and love.

Reflection: The beauty of using process drama in teaching synthesis is that the process of being in the role of a character from a story works beautifully for children who are attentive to the most distinguishing features of a character and able to imitate them. In their book *Imagining to Learn: Inquiry, Ethics, and Integration Through Drama*, Jeffrey Wilhelm and Brian Edmiston (1998) describe how "in drama, the imaginative cocreation of the story world is made visible. Students can work together to create meaning, and then step outside the drama world to monitor how, why, and how well they did so" (p. 32). This action of re-creating the character helped our students develop and extend their characters into new actions and events, which ultimately helped them synthesize their own thoughts and feelings with those of the characters and the author to build a deeper meaning of the text.

Using *Querencias* to Build a Cohesive Whole

Grades: 4–5

Materials: wood pieces (give each student one wood piece 6" × 8" and two wood pieces 3" × 8"); leather scraps; collage materials, such as paints, beads, buttons, dried flowers, tiny shells and rocks, ribbon, postcards, wrapping paper, and fabric; magazines (for cutting); glue; scissors

Text Resource: *Journey of the Sparrows* (Buss, 1993)

Lesson: After our fifth-grade book club finished its last book for the year, *Journey of the Sparrows*, students met for their final discussion and art project. Fran Buss's book tells the story of 15-year-old Maria as she travels illegally from El Salvador to Chicago, Illinois, USA. The book details her struggle to survive and how her talent for drawing provides her with financial support and shelter during her journey. The book club had been very special to us, and we wanted to make a piece that would represent our synthesis of what had been important to us in our reading. Therefore, we chose to construct a collage on wood called a *querencia*, meaning "a place for the heart" (McMann, 1998, p. 14). *Querencias* come from the Latin tradition of building special places to honor ancestors, loved ones, or special occasions. The *querencia* is meant to be a secret place in which the doors can be opened and shared with others, or closed and private. Each student began by taking three pieces of wood and attaching them with leather so the two smaller pieces would open as doors to reveal the inside—the student's heartfelt feelings (see Appendix B for specific instructions on making *querencias*).

Next, students searched through magazines to find words that might express what the books had taught them. There were squeals of excitement as students found and called out these words. Daniella was first to share her findings, "Listen to this: 'Nothing feels better than staring down your fears.'" She told us that she thought this phrase said a lot about the girls in the books and how they faced life. This comment led to a discussion of our own fears and how we avoided or dealt with them. "I have the word that says it all," shouted Maya. We all looked up to see her holding up the word *hope*.

We also provided materials to remind students of the books' characters, as well as the characters' problems and hopes. For example, students had sand to remind them of Billie Joe's blizzards of dust, fake gold to remember Anna's lost power in Byzantium, and one of Hughes's poems from *Dave at Night* (Levine, 1999). Collage materials such as paints, beads, shells, and rocks also were provided. Each student designed her *querencia* with the idea of presenting one powerful image or idea made up of her own personal collection of paintings, photos, and mementos. Each *querencia* took on the unique qualities of each girl. Rachel's *querencia* had words like *dream* and *take a risk*. Maya chose the central spot in her *querencia* for the words *listen to your inner voice*. We asked each girl to think of a metaphor for what she had learned from the characters in the books. Rachel wrote the following to go with the mountain photos on her *querencia*:

> In the beginning of the books, everything would be fine for the characters, then they'd fall off the cliff. The fall would be the worst part. But after that thay'd [*sic*] swim to shore and climb the mountain agan [*sic*]. I learned that I could do that too, when I have a problem.

Finally, reminded of how the characters had a passion for art, piano, or writing that helped them survive, we asked the students to share how their passions gave them strength. Maya, for example, said, "When I have a problem, I can write about it in my journal, and when I finish, I feel so much cleaner!" As we finished this final project, we sent them off to middle school with wishes for strength and hope and were confident that they had tools to help them listen to their inner voices.

Reflection: The process of collage challenged students to use their spatial intelligence. The ability to see and produce a graphic likeness of spatial information allowed students to find the words to describe this similarity. We discovered how many children were sustained and challenged by visual images before they had the words to describe them. For some students, the process of collage enhanced their learning process, whereas others needed this experience to show us the best of their thinking.

Using Mural Painting to Discover Relevant Truth

Grades: 3–5

Materials: large canvas or other painting surface, acrylic paints or discounted latex paints, brushes, buckets of water

Text Resource: *Wings* (Myers, 2000)

Lesson: During their recess, our fourth graders were faced with a playground problem that overwhelmed us all. This problem occurred only days after the shootings at the high school in Columbine, Colorado, which was only 45 minutes away from our own school. Along with the rest of the United States, we were reeling. But our students' discussion of the name-calling and teasing that took place on our playground led them to the bigger question: How does violence come about in schools? The children seemed to be asking all the important questions, sensing that what they were dealing with was connected to a bigger picture.

Because ours was a focus school, we shared space with a neighborhood school, which had been more than gracious in hosting us in their building. However, our schools seemed quite different at times, and children in both schools noticed this difference. Staff members at both schools were aware that this created tension, and we always were working toward helping children get to know and respect one another.

Children in the neighborhood school must have been puzzled by the format of our work sometimes, and on this day in particular, they expressed this concern with name-calling: "You kids are dummies. You never do any work. You're all 'artsy fartsy.'" Our students were puzzled by this hostility. They felt that they worked pretty hard and wondered, "What's wrong with art anyway?" One student, Sandra, asked, "And besides, why do they have to trip us when they're teasing us like that?" Oscar asked, "Why can't they just play soccer?" Meanwhile, the neighborhood schoolchildren complained about our students not playing fair, not listening to their complaints, and not taking them seriously.

In the first days after the Columbine shootings, our students were thinking hard. They engaged in profound discussions about the kinds of things that separate people at school. Students could see how teasing might lead to intense anger. They were beginning to understand that when different people do not know one another very well, they can make all kinds of assumptions about one another. Students even were able to take responsibility for some of their own behavior. In short, they were making a variety of connections in their discussions.

Our students thought it was important to meet with and talk to the fourth graders from the neighborhood school, so we invited them to our school for refreshments and conversation. Students from both schools began to unravel a long cord of misunderstanding and weave a new cord of understanding. They did not solve all their problems, but afterward, students could at least get on with playing soccer. Within the context of this playground problem solving, the children were able to discuss similar incidents in our community, such as the time the black student committee at a local university was getting hate mail. They also talked about the biases they noticed toward children who were African American and Hispanic American, and the girls talked about ways they were treated differently on the sports field. As a result of these discussions, students decided that they wanted everyone to walk into our school and know that this was a place where everyone should be respected.

To help the students reach this goal and to develop their thinking further, Roberta read the book *Wings*, the story of a boy who can fly. When he tries to attend school, other students tease him because he is different. We chose this book because of its familiar theme, which we thought would allow students to make connections to the text easily and ultimately help them synthesize all their thoughts from the discussions and the text into a coherent thought.

After students read the book, we asked them to create a message to paint on a mural that would show the result of their understandings about honoring diversity. Students began painting first and asked children from different classes to be models for their mural so it would reflect our school. They used brightly colored acrylic paints to begin painting their vision on a mural. After completing their painting, all the students said it felt like the children in the mural were flowers in a garden, so the words for their statement began to form. They wanted it to reflect their strong opinions about teasing, but they chose to make it as hopeful as they felt. After a great deal of conversation, planning, and negotiating, they finally invented their own antibias statement—"We are one beautiful garden made up of many radiant flowers. We will not tolerate the weeds of discrimination!" After students painted their statement on the mural, they hung it on the wall by the front door of our building so that everyone who entered the school could see it (see Figure 21). This activity showed us that life is complicated for children, too, but when given time and support, they can sort it out in a meaningful way.

Reflection: In this lesson, there were many supporting conversations with students that helped bring them to their work of synthesis. However, it was the challenge of proclaiming their ideas in a concise art form that helped them create the final fusion of thoughts, feelings, and experiences. In our

Figure 21   Fourth Graders' Antibias Mural

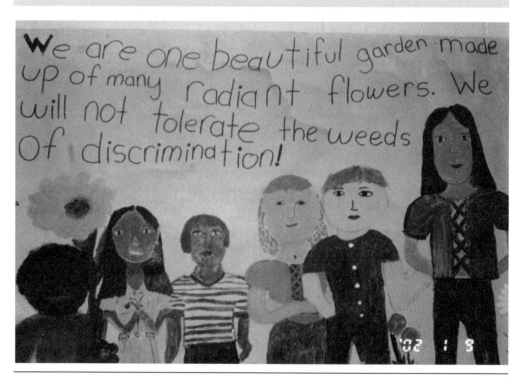

work with children, we often saw the visual image come first as a solution to a problem. This visual synthesis then sparked the students' discussion. This process also could be used to assess the learning of children who have limited English or who have problems processing language. Looking at the visual images that children produce as a result of synthesizing text and personal experience is a powerful way to assess learning when these children are not ready to talk or write about their ideas.

Using Montage to Discover Commonalities in Research

Grades: 1–2

Materials: Heavyweight paper (poster size), scissors, glue, drawings, photos or magazine photos

Text Resource: *The Salamander Room* (Mazer, 1991)

Lesson: First graders were involved in an animal study when their teacher, Suzanne, asked us to work with a small group of students on synthesis. We were going to read *The Salamander Room*, the story of a young boy who finds a salamander and wants it to live with him. Questions in the text help the boy mentally design a habitat for the salamander, which involves remodeling his room until he is living with the salamander and sleeping "on a bed under the stars, with the moon shining through the green leaves of the trees" (n.p.). We decided to use this book to help students merge information they had learned from their firsthand observations of salamanders with information they had learned about bats from a recent school visit from a bat expert. Our goal was to support students in seeing the similarities between these divergent animals and similarities in the study of them. We used the book to help encourage comparisons of animal studies.

Because this was during the first months of first grade, the children's enthusiasm for scientific research surpassed their writing abilities; therefore, we decided to use a montage of drawings to illustrate synthesis. As students read *The Salamander Room* to themselves silently, they easily recognized that the text structure—with its questions and answers—helped them identify the kinds of things salamanders need to survive, such as shelter, food, and water. But because this is a fiction text, it lends itself to less scientific answers such as "Salamanders need friends to play with!" In these cases, we talked with students about their observations of the salamanders in the classroom. After the read-aloud, we asked children to draw pictures of the things salamanders needed. They drew pictures of insects and worms to represent salamander food and pools of water, rocks, and leaves for salamander shelter. We then glued their pictures onto a poster, creating a montage with a salamander in the middle.

After our bat expert left, we asked students to draw pictures of what bats need to survive. They drew pictures of insects and pools of water and caves to represent bat food and shelter, respectively. When all the drawings had been glued to a poster to create a bat montage, we asked students to compare the two montages. As they examined their work, they began waving their hands and told us, "They both need insects, they both need water, they could even both live in a cave!"

Reflection: After students made comparisons, we then created the beginnings of a Venn diagram by recording these similarities in the middle of the two montages. However, the montage was a more appropriate model for students at this age, because their reading and writing abilities were just emerging. Montage provided an inclusive model in which all children could participate while they honed their reading, writing, and science skills. This art form also would be helpful to students learning English as a second language (ESL), allowing them to articulate their learning through the montage before they learn the vocabulary to express their thinking verbally. In *Visual Literacy: Learn to See, See to Learn*, Lynell Burmark (2002) observes that visual literacy is an important resource for teachers of students learning ESL. The students' discovery of the similarities between salamanders and bats also led them to important generalizations that helped build a foundation for further scientific research. Children who have a strong naturalist intelligence, who thrive on observing and classifying living things in nature, will be especially interested in learning about synthesis through this lesson. You also could do this study with your students using any number of different animals and fiction and nonfiction texts.

Final Thoughts

The quality of the arts that we appreciate is the many ways that artists synthesize intellect, emotion, and intelligence into one piece of dance, drama, painting, or music. This appreciation has influenced our understanding of comprehension. This chapter showed how the arts became a model for us as we taught children how reading comprehension depends on a reader's ability to synthesize these very same pieces as he or she reads. We found that children readily use their bodies, minds, and emotions to fuse their thoughts about the meaning of text.

Chapter 8

Case Studies of Students With Learning Difficulties

There are two types of education:
one that teaches how to make
a living and the one that teaches
how to live. You all know which
type of education the arts support.

—Marie Emmitt, 1998, p. 3

Megan, a third grader, strides into the classroom, with her backpack hanging off her shoulders, her hair whipping around her face, and her journal outstretched in her hands. She says, "Sabine, read this poem; I just finished it."

> The wind is blowing the grass.
> Wind settled and blowing
> But still spring is here
> Could the trees be talking?

Even though writing is profoundly difficult for Megan, she sees herself as a poet and songwriter. Megan cannot write a long story, but the concise formats of poetry and songwriting—which she often uses—allow her to communicate her passion for life. Like all students with learning difficulties, she yearns to be recognized and heard by those around her. Through the arts, we see the depth of Megan's thinking.

Awakening Students' Passion With the Arts

When we began our journey using the arts to help students learn reading comprehension strategies, we had multiple reasons for trying this approach. But, as previously noted, one reason stood out: We believed that the teaching approaches we had been using were not reaching some students. Some of these children had been struggling academically for a long time, and at times, their methods of learning seemed mysterious. However, we noticed that when they were involved in the arts they often became different children. All of a sudden, students who were previously quiet and hard to reach during reading time shined as they participated in class discussions and shared their thoughts with others. This chapter will explore how some of these students grew through different arts activities and will celebrate students' unique ways of learning.

Using a Multisensory Approach With Jessie, a Student With Cognitive and Emotional Learning Challenges

When Jessie, a second grader, opened the door of Sabine's classroom, we were never sure who would be there to greet us—a ballet dancer, cat, police officer, or some other character who had sparked her imagination. At recess, she was either in charge of the class tetherball or on the basketball court trying to make a shot. Jessie also had multiple cognitive and emotional learning challenges because of brain damage and developmental delays, respectively, which made the process of learning and being connected to her grade-level peers extremely difficult. Like most students, she loved having the spotlight on her when she knew she had something to share. However, as she got older, finding those opportunities became more difficult. It became challenging for us to create whole-group instruction that was meaningful for her, as well as for the other students. Because Jessie also was hearing impaired, she relied on visual cues more than most students and had difficulty following more complicated stories and discussions. Using the arts to teach reading comprehension strategies helped Jessie become a participating member of the class, as well as learn some basic aspects of reading comprehension.

We first saw Jessie make strides in her learning when she participated in a poetry-movement exercise. In her class, one of our daily rituals was reading a poem each morning. We accompanied the reading with movement that accentuated different aspects of the text. Each morning when Jessie joined the circle, her body moved with the whole class and her words loudly joined us for the more significant phrases in the poems. By including movement in this ritual, we enabled Jessie to follow our speech and develop an understanding of some aspects of the text.

We observed Jessie become focused and involved during our class investigation into questioning as a reading comprehension strategy. When the class listened to music of whales singing, Jessie wondered what animal was making those sounds. She never asked a question when listening to a book or a story in class, so this was a big step. During our investigation, we then went from having students generate questions around a piece of music to having them read, with the focus on generating questions. Jessie went to her book box (each child kept a book box in the classroom that included both teacher- and student-selected books) and pulled out a pile of very short books. She was not yet reading words but did know how to hold a book, turn the pages, and look at pictures. Jessie chose to look through a book about superheroes. When we returned to the circle and students started to share their questions, Jessie raised her hand and asked, "Why does Superman fly?" She also showed the class the page in the book that made her think of this question. We believed that by having Jessie first ask questions about the music, we had helped her to create a question about the book.

Later in the year, students in Jessie's class participated in an arts lesson meant to teach them inferring. During this lesson, each student created a sock doll to represent his or her heroic self. Jessie created a beautiful doll that had feathers coming out of its head, a cape, and a mask. When she shared her creation with the students, she spoke of how the feathers on her doll represented her dream to fly. By having Jessie represent one of her dreams in a physical model, we allowed her to enter the class's study of this reading comprehension strategy.

Having the opportunity to see a student like Jessie share with the class and join our activities and discussions in a meaningful manner was an unforeseen gift of using the arts. We had worked with Jessie for two years, and it was only through using the arts that she finally revealed herself as a learner to us and the class.

Using Drawing With Alex, a Resistant Reader

"Do I have to do this? I know that I am never going to think of any connections," Alex moaned privately one day when we began our language arts time. Then, we showed him the six prints we had placed in isolated places in his second-grade classroom. Alex grabbed his clipboard, paper, and pencil and joined his group. Students within each group were writing down the connections they made to one print, then moving on to the next print. Alex was quiet and focused as he worked. The list on his paper was growing quickly. In fact, when this viewing time was over, he told his neighbor, "I have 28 connections." Alex easily made connections to the prints, especially one flower print that reminded him of the flowers in his garden.

Alex loved art: He brought paintings to class that he had made at home, donated art materials, and spent weeks perfecting a certain picture. He also showed attention to detail, noticing small changes we made to the class environment and always being the first student to spot a new haircut or pair of shoes or earrings. But Alex was very resistant to any language arts activities, which included class read-aloud time. Alex was a good student, and there was no apparent reason why he was having a difficult time learning how to read.

As the year progressed, we saw a strong correlation between Alex's level of engagement in reading and the amount of art we used in our lessons. After the students had developed their ability to use questioning through a variety of art and text experiences, Alex became a leader in asking probing questions during read-alouds. For example, while reading a biography of John Muir, Alex pondered why Muir would have a grizzly-bear blanket if he was a naturalist. Alex's reliance on the arts to help develop meaning continued throughout the year. Near the end of our Amazon study, which we had used to teach students about sensory imagery, we decided to turn the classroom into the rain forest and the Amazon River. We thought students were ready to interact with text without using the arts. In each area of the river, therefore, we had placed a different piece of writing that required the students to activate many different sensory images in order to develop their comprehension of the piece. Some of the writing was poetry, although other pieces were nonfiction descriptive passages.

Alex picked up his clipboard and sat in front of the poem "Tree's Place" (George, 1998b), which describes how a tree is anchored to the ground and claims a space for itself: "Within this space, all belongs to Tree / Turf, shaft of air, even slices of sun" (p. 25). He sat very still, looking up at the poem, but his pen was not moving. When we asked Alex what he was thinking, he replied, "Nothing. I can't think of anything." Then, Roberta read aloud the poem to help him. Alex then wrote, "I picture the rain forest; when you plant a tree it stays there." This statement had more to do with his background knowledge of rain forests than his understanding of the poem. Because we knew that art was so useful to Alex, we asked if he would like to draw a picture of this poem first. We specifically asked him to describe what the poem would look like. Alex was eager to get started, so he got some pastels and went right to work.

When he was done, he shared his picture with us (see Figure 22), and we asked him to explain why he had drawn some of the different parts. Alex explained that the roots were what held the tree in place and that the red lines on top of the tree were the shafts of air that go to the tree because the tree will not move. He also told us that the tree owned the air and was big in the middle because it was not going anywhere. Written and oral communication about the poem had felt insurmountable, although artwork had allowed Alex to explain his image and comprehension of the poem. This experience with Alex deepened our commitment to using the arts to bring more students into the learning process.

Using Music and Art With Adam, a Twice-Exceptional Student

Adam was a naturalist. If we started talking to him about animals such as bats, he would tell us about all the different types of bats and give us a detailed analysis of how bats used echolocation (the use of sound waves to locate objects) to find food. Adam often brought very sophisticated books to his first-grade class to have read aloud. He was a twice-exceptional student, who was brilliant in many areas but had an extremely difficult time sitting, focusing, and learning rudimentary skills.

Often, it was difficult to know what to do for Adam; that is, we wanted to keep him interested and engaged in learning, yet we knew he had to learn how to read, write, and become mathematically literate. Adam was a beginning reader, so no book that he might be able to read would provide him any challenge in the area of comprehension. Through the arts, we were able to challenge Adam to use the comprehension strategies and build an understanding of what they were. Even though he is still struggling in his development as a reader, we hope that when he becomes a fluent reader, he already will be comfortable using the strategies.

Using the arts gave us a new tool to help Adam develop reading comprehension strategies. When our lessons included music or painting, Adam was an active participant with significant insights. As we listened to *Pacific Blue* (Schramm, 1993) during our questioning study, Adam (a second grader by this time) created a list of questions, ranging from "What animal is that?" to "How were they able to tape the music and whales together?" He enjoyed listening to the music and was able to focus and work independently. Throughout our work, whenever we used the arts to teach and model the strategies and ways of thinking, Adam was able to shine and share with the class much of what he knew.

Using Drama With Ori, a Student Learning English as a Second Language (ESL)

Ori is one of those students who immediately caught our eyes in the hall. He was cute as a button and at times, seemed full of life and smiles. But other times, he was howling—on the playground, in the hall, or often in the classroom. In class, we saw him pinching the person sitting next to him regularly. Ori was a first grader who worked with the ESL teacher sharing a room with Roberta, so the ESL teacher and Roberta often got to talk about their students. Because the ESL teacher also was a practicing visual artist, she was eager to have us use the arts to build reading comprehension with her students. Weekly, we worked with Ori and other students in a library research group.

Ori had been in the United States for a year. Originally from Israel, he was struggling to learn English. However, Ori struggled more than most students learning English as a second language because he also was hearing impaired. He wore hearing aids in both ears and was learning American Sign Language in addition to English.

One afternoon, Ori and the other students were in the middle of a research project on Alaskan animals. The librarian was modeling how to organize research from a book about musk oxen. The class was very excited; Ori was pinching the student next to him, Leslie. After Roberta read and discussed this book with the children, and after the librarian showed them how to use a web to organize their information, we asked the children to write about musk oxen in small groups. The American Sign Language interpreter was helping Ori to do his work. Roberta caught her eye, and the interpreter raised her eyebrows as if to say, "We're doing our best here but getting nowhere." Therefore, we suggested that we take Ori and his small group outside for a little process drama. The students showed interest, so we found an open spot in a field outside.

We introduced the activity by dividing the group into two smaller groups containing musk oxen and wolves. The musk oxen were either calves, mothers, or bulls. We reminded students how in the book we had read, the musk oxen circle around their young to protect them when wolves attack, and we asked them to interpret this action. The object of this drama game was to capture the ribbon that the wolves or calves were wearing. The interpreter signed our directions for Ori.

In the drama, Ori first played a calf. He sat on the ground and covered his eyes with his hands. When the wolves attacked, he was giggling nervously. During the next wolf attack, he was a bull, whose job was to defeat and send away the wolves. This time, Ori focused intently on his task and moved furiously to win over a wolf, but to no avail. The wolf won, and Ori had to sit on the sidelines. He spent this time howling. On the last try, Ori played a wolf. He and the other wolves gathered behind a cottonwood tree planning their strategy. Then, the wolves attacked the musk oxen, and Ori managed to capture the ribbon of a calf. The victory clearly pleased him, as evidenced by the look on his face.

When we returned to the library to write, it was apparent that Ori had a stronger grip on the events described in the book on musk oxen. He was able to write furiously for 15 minutes before it was time for the class to go. Indeed, we have found that the use of drama or puppetry in teaching students learning ESL helps them internalize language and content. It was clear from this drama game that the additional layers of active participation—with gestures, movement, and role-play—helped Ori scaffold the book's content. Process drama can be a bridge to understanding that takes only a few minutes of classroom time but makes a huge difference for children struggling to understand a new language, as well as new ideas.

Using Construction With Cole, a Student With Emotional Challenges

Cole came to our school as a second grader. He reportedly disliked school intensely, was not cooperative with adults, and had a history of physically aggressive behavior with other children. During the past year he had not completed any assigned work; therefore, his goal for the coming year was to complete some of it.

We worked with Cole on multiple levels and believed that it was a combination of the work of many staff members, a myriad of meetings, and a variety of approaches that really supported his learning growth. But one key piece that stood out for us after the year had ended was bridge building. Cole's reading was almost at grade level when we met him, which was surprising because he rarely picked up a book and never finished reading one. His comprehension was poor, and he could not maintain any commitment to figuring out challenging text. We realized the affect of bridge building on Cole's learning because by the end of the year, he was at least a fan of non-fiction, especially books about bridges.

We introduced bridge building early in the year with a book titled *The Brooklyn Bridge* (Mann, 1996). Students constructed bridges with their bodies, paper and straws, and wooden blocks. Then, we bought a K'NEX bridge-building kit for the class. Cole's life took a turn for the better from that day on. We designated a special bridge-building area in our room, and Cole took refuge there when he needed time apart from the frustrations of school. Cole also built more bridges than the other students and kept a journal of the drawings of bridges he had built and the ones he had designed but not yet constructed (see Figure 23 for an example of one of these drawings). When the

Figure 23   Cole's Journal Drawing of a Bridge

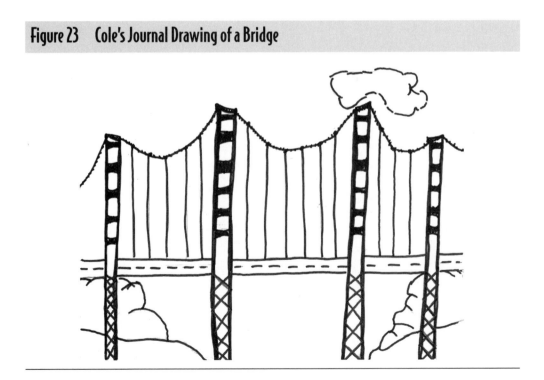

rest of the class had moved onto weaving, Cole was still building bridges. By weaving long pieces of wool for his suspension bridges, he even found a way to integrate weaving with his bridge construction. Cole asked us if he could do more work, stay after school, and take the bridge books home for the weekend or on his vacation. Clearly, he had met the learning goal that we had set with him at the beginning of the year.

Cole's enthusiasm for learning grew until the end of the year, when he became a self-described naturalist and lover of owls, a weaver, a historian of ancient cultures, and an intrepid mathematician who specialized in challenging problems. So was it the arts that built Cole's reading comprehension and love for school? We thought the arts certainly played a big part.

Final Thoughts

This chapter demonstrated how the arts can be so compelling that children allow themselves to be inexorably drawn into both art and books. Once drawn in, children learn a certain amount of industry from the arts that they then can apply to their comprehension of text. For instance, it takes patience to build a suspension bridge, just as it takes patience to ask questions about text. It takes time to weave a suspension bridge, just as it takes time to stop and make predictions or inferences. Cole can build and weave and ask questions and make predictions and inferences. Because we used the arts to teach reading comprehension strategies, Cole is both an artist and a reader.

Throughout this project, it was often the students who struggled with learning the most that showed us the power of the arts. Much of school learning focuses on only auditory or visual learning, so it is often difficult for students with learning challenges to find ways to express their thinking. However, they can compensate for their difficulties by learning through another intelligence, such as musical or kinesthetic. By giving students with learning difficulties the chance to became a musk ox, build a bridge, or draw a tree, we enabled them to learn and express themselves in ways that highlighted their way of knowing.

For some students with learning difficulties, school also provides a strenuous social atmosphere that causes them to reject learning. The arts add elements of accessibility, confidence building, and enjoyment that can change a student's feelings about learning. As teachers, the arts enabled us to see beyond students' limitations by showing us all their possibilities.

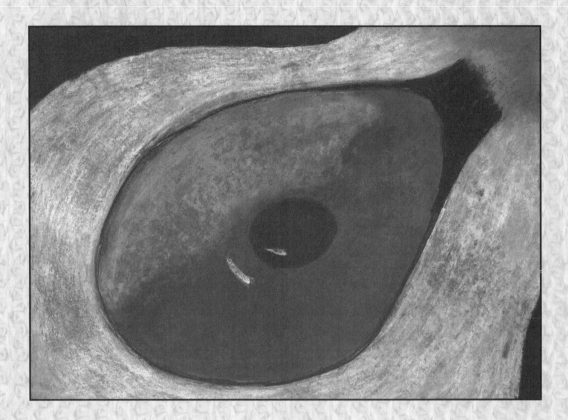

Chapter 9

Assessment of Students' Reading Comprehension

When we teach a child to draw,
we teach him how to see.
When we teach a child to play a musical instrument,
we teach her how to listen.
When we teach a child how to dance,
we teach him how to move through life with grace.
When we teach a child how to read or write,
we teach her how to think.
When we nurture imagination,
we create a better world, one child at a time.

—Jane Alexander (as cited in Cornett, 1998, p. 79)

Jan's fifth graders are in the library bent over *National Geographic* photographs with their paper viewfinders. Students are trying to identify the most intriguing piece of nature from each photograph. They are looking specifically for colors, textures, patterns, and designs that they can enlarge in a drawing. Some students spot the eye of a toucan or the feather of a goose. Other students see beauty and pattern in the edge of a leaf or the spiral of a shell. The goal is for students to demonstrate their knowledge of Georgia O'Keefe's style of painting. Each student takes this small patch of nature and enlarges it as O'Keefe did with her paintings of flowers and bones. Later, when we visit the fifth-grade classroom after the students have completed their paintings, we are caught off guard by the nature portraits that fill the wall. The toucan's eye startles, the goose's feather intrigues, and the leaf dazzles. These students had turned their small discoveries into powerful pieces of art.

These small discoveries were what we looked for when we observed children talking or writing about their reading. For instance, a child's discovery about a character or the pattern of events may turn into an epiphany about the story. In this moment, the child weaves together all the strands of his or her thinking about the story into a rich fabric of understanding. When children made discoveries, we were startled by their ability to think deeply and honestly. We found ourselves listening with a new ear to children's conversations. The stories we collected from students were about insights into their thinking. The questions we reflected on with students were about comprehension: What sorts of inferences were they making, how did they synthesize an idea like that, and where did they draw their wisdom for that kind of advice? Asking these types of questions helped us to deepen our own observations and thinking about children's learning.

As teachers, we are fascinated with the ways children think about the world. In this chapter, you will find some ways to assess children's thinking as they use reading comprehension strategies. However, we constantly are reminded that written assessments and writing assignments are not the only forms of assessment. We believe that "Instead, everything from the kinds of tasks that have been assigned to the way the classroom has been organized is intended to help the teacher know as much as possible about how students are making sense of things" (Kohn, 2000, p. 41).

We learn more about children's thinking when we look at their work in a variety of ways over time. The assessments discussed in this chapter will offer opportunities to view students' thinking as they use reading-response logs, book club responses, and double-entry journals. Also included in this chapter are Arts Observation Guides, which we use as teacher tools for monitoring students' use of comprehension strategies through the arts. Appendix C provides blackline masters of some of the assessments discussed in this chapter.

Using Teacher Observation to Assess Students' Use of Strategies

We provided a variety of opportunities for children to show their thinking about their reading. Some methods we used were reading-response logs, book clubs, individual student-teacher reading conferences, and whole-class and small-group discussions about shared books. When we used these methods, our roles as teachers were to recognize when to ask the question that would give us insight into a student's level of comprehension. We also watched for clues that would tell us whether students were making meaning of the text. For example, in a recent response to a poem about seeing the stars, one child saw the word *skyscraper* and immediately jumped to a discussion of the tragedy of September 11, 2001. Our observations allowed us to note that although this child was able to make connections to one idea in the poem, he lost the meaning of the poem as whole.

Observing children using the arts provided us with additional opportunities to identify their use of the strategies to make meaning. Using the Arts Observation Guides in Appendix C (see pages 171–175), we have identified elements of construction, dance and movement, drama, music, and visual arts to guide our observations and subsequent assessments. Using these guides, we first looked for evidence of arts elements in children's work, then looked for ways they used the arts to express meaning about the text. We often focused on one strategy at a time, but as children's knowledge and use of the strategies grow, they may be using multiple strategies in one art lesson. Figure 24 is a sample of a completed Arts Observation Guide for Dance and Movement.

Name: Hanna

Date: October 18

Art-Based Activity: Jazz Dance

Comprehension Strategy: Developing schema for unfamiliar text structure

Evidence of Arts Elements	Arts Elements	Evidence of Meaning Making
Hanna is very expressive.	**Body** Communicates, controls, and expresses rhythms and tempo	Hanna used her body to communicate various rhythms indicated in the text.
	Energy Demonstrates strong flow, appropriate energy, and mood	Hanna used her energy in dance to share her ideas about the change in the text.
	Communication Problem solves and uses symbolism	Hanna easily translated her ideas about the text to a kinesthetic expression in dance.
Hanna improvises freely and uses a variety of levels and shapes to express herself.	**Choreography** Improvises and shows variety in use of space, levels, and shapes	Hanna has a repertoire of dance schema to bring to her interpretation of the text.
Hanna is very engaged in this activity and obviously sees herself as a dancer.	**Focus** Concentrates, shows engagement, and follows directions	

Observations and comments: Hanna is a real leader in using dance to express ideas, encouraging other children to participate seriously.

Using Students' Written Responses to Assess Their Use of Strategies and Reading Comprehension

There is a continuum of reading-response formats that teachers use for assessment. These formats vary from reading-response logs, book club responses, poetry responses, double-entry journals, graphic organizers, and students' other written responses to specific questions for literacy portfolios or graded assignments. The common thread in all these responses is the teacher's expectation to elicit thinking from students based on their use of reading comprehension strategies.

Blackline masters of book club responses such as artful artist, connector, discussion director, investigator, literary luminary, and travel tracer (pages 176–181); a double-entry journal (page 182); and a reading-response log (page 184) are included in Appendix C. Teachers can use book club responses when working with groups of students reading the same book. The teacher gives each member of the group a job or role, such as literary luminary, then at the weekly book club meeting, members share from the viewpoint of their different roles. The double-entry journal format offers teachers the ability to see students' responses to specific selections of text whether the teacher or student makes the selection. When teachers choose complex pieces of text, this enables them to check students' use of reading comprehension strategies. When students select meaningful pieces of text, this shows teachers students' level of interaction with text because it demonstrates why the pieces are meaningful for students and what comprehension strategies they are using to gain meaning. A reading-response log allows students to provide a more independent and personal written response as they reflect about what they are reading. At times, teachers may guide students' responses by asking them to focus on one element of the story or one reading comprehension strategy.

Because most of our third graders had a great deal of exposure to learning about the strategies, we chose to use written responses as an indication of how fluent these students were in using the strategies in the context of content area reading. During the third-grade class study on Colorado history, students read poetry, nonfiction, and fiction from the point of view of Native Americans, slaves, women, mountain men, miners, and pioneers. Several times during the study, we checked in with students through written responses to monitor their use of the strategies. The following example illustrates how students were able to spontaneously use comprehension strategies to gain meaning from the wealth of ideas that were being shared. Sara's reading-response log about Mary Stahler's poem "A Pioneer Woman Looks Back" (as cited in Katz, 2000) is a rich example of her ability to build and activate schema, develop sensory images, use inferential thinking, and synthesize the poem to gain a personalized, intricate understanding of the piece. Her response to this poem (Figure 25), about a pioneer woman's lament over moving to the prairie, also illustrated to us how students were able to use comprehension strategies independently to gain meaning from the wealth of ideas being shared in the text.

Figure 25   Sara's Written Response to "A Pioneer Woman Looks Back"

1. What was your response to this poem, what did it make you think about, wonder about or feel?

> It made me think about having to leave my home. It made me wonder why you would choose land over family. I could feel the wind whistling in my ears, because that is probaly what you would hear most.

2. The author uses the phrase, **"endless land............endless sky"** four or five times in this poem. What do you think she means by the saying?

> She's saying that there's no end to the land and no end to the sky. It's a long journey.

3. At the end of the poem what do you think the characters feelings are about the move?

> I think they loved where they used to live. They might have felt lonely. They felt they payed a price when they moved.

Using Observation to Assess Students' Overall Growth in Comprehension

As we honed our observation skills, we also gathered evidence of students' thinking to document how they had grown in their ability to use the strategies to gain comprehension. We used the Observation Checklist to Look for Evidence of Growth in Comprehension (see page 183) to help guide our observation of students during a variety of literacy-based activities, such as small-group discussions, writing in reading-response logs, or dramatic interviews. Our observations were based on elements of each comprehension strategy. We looked for the depth and quality of students' thinking rather than simply their ability to use the language of the strategies. Figure 26 provides an example of a completed observation. This observation of Ana, a fourth-grade student, was done after she wrote a story about her grandfather using ideas

Figure 26
Sample of Completed Observation Checklist to Look for Evidence of Growth in Comprehension

Name: Ana   **Date:** November 5

Book Title: _Ghost Wings_ and _Pablo Remembers: The Fiesta of the Day of the Dead_

Art Project: (circle one) Whole-class discussion   Small-group discussion

⟨Reading-response log⟩   Art activity

Strategy	**Evidence From Child's Response**
Developing Sensory Images	
• Makes pictures in mind	
• Uses multiple senses	"I remember...the smell of sawdust and cigars."
• Includes an emotional component	
• Adds detail through imagery	
• Develops a mental model to organize meaning	
Building and Activating Schema	
• Makes text-to-self connections	"If I was carrying a Day of the Dead basket...."
• Makes text-to-text connections	
• Makes text-to-world connections	"The little girl...remembered roses....
• Uses connections to build meaning	I remember sawdust."
Questioning	
• Asks yes or no questions	
• Asks higher level questions	
• Asks questions to clarify author's intent	
• Uses questioning to evolve in his or her thinking	
Determining Importance	
• Distinguishes between details and essential ideas	
• Recognizes important themes	"If I was carrying a Day of the Dead basket...."
Inferring	
• Communicates emotional content of text	
• Has insight into the characters and events of story	"The memories make me happy...."
• Makes predictions based on inferences of text	
• Creates a personal interpretation	
• Discovers author's implied messages	
Synthesis	
• Creates a summary of the text	
• Discovers commonalities in texts	"The little girl in _Ghost Wings_ remembered her grandma by the smell of cornmeal and roses. I remember my Grandpa Bill by the smell of sawdust and cigars."
• Generates new meaning based on author's ideas and own personal interpretations	

in her reading-response log. The particular response from which she drew her ideas focused on books read during a small-group reading of *Ghost Wings* (Joosse, 2001) and *Pablo Remembers: The Fiesta of the Day of the Dead* (Ancona, 1993). These books shared ideas about losing grandparents and ways that family members are remembered during Day of the Dead celebrations in Mexico. We made a copy of Ana's story, which follows, and attached it to the checklist to keep in her literacy portfolio.

Grandpa Bill

By Ana

Grandpa Bill was very close to my heart. He used to call me Tiger, and then he would growl. One night he held me on his lap and told me he would miss me. I didn't know what he meant. That night I overheard my mom and my aunt talking. Grandpa Bill had died. I think that my grandpa knew that he was going to die pretty soon.

I'm going to miss bowling with my grandpa. He taught me how to put my first three fingers in the holes of the ball and PUSH it down the alley. I liked to bowl so much he bought me my own bowling set. He had his own bowling ball. I thought that was neat because not many people have their own bowling ball. I think of Grandpa Bill whenever I go to a bowling alley and make a strike!

My grandpa liked to invent things. He had a shop in the garage with all the tools he used. He had saws and hammers and goggles and other machines to invent things with. He was an engineer, and he liked to fix things that were broken. He was good at that.

On the Day of the Dead celebration, you can communicate with the spirits of people who have died. If I could talk to Grandpa Bill one more time, I would feel so happy. If I was carrying a Day of the Dead basket to his favorite places, I would first go the bowling alley. I would put a cigar in the basket because he liked cigars. The little girl in *Ghost Wings* remembered her grandma by the smell of cornmeal and roses. I remember my Grandpa Bill by the smell of sawdust and cigars. The memories make me happy, but I still miss my grandpa.

Literacy Portfolios

We used the literacy portfolio to gather various evidence of each child's growth over time and then share it with parents. Reviewing the literacy portfolio with parents and children was always a delightful process as we looked over past work and identified the many ways children were thinking and growing. Parents learned more about their children's thinking and our teaching as they looked through a portfolio with us. Elements of student work within a literacy portfolio might include

- a photo of a tableau with a response,
- a painting with a description,
- a poem and a reflection,
- a drawing with a key to understanding,
- a transcript of a dramatic interview,
- a song written in response to text,
- a photo or drawing of a model in blocks or sand, or
- reading-response logs or stories.

Also included in these portfolios were anecdotal evidence or reflections from book club discussions.

Because students were able to share deeper understandings about stories through the arts, it was important to document and save these artifacts and moments in literacy portfolios.

District and State Assessments

Twice a year, teachers in our school district use district-chosen, secured benchmark books to assess all students in grades K–2. These books are not used for teaching; therefore, they are new texts for children. The testing includes a running record on the text, as well as prepared comprehension questions. In grades 3–5, teachers in our district use the Qualitative Reading Inventory (QRI) to test for decoding and comprehension abilities. Recent assessments of students in grades K–2 and grades 3–5 (using benchmark books and the QRI, respectively) showed only three children in our school struggled with comprehension, indicated by missing more than one question on their tests.

For several years, our school has participated in statewide testing, the Colorado State Assessment Program, that measures reading progress. Students at our school have done particularly well on the reading comprehension portion of the test, scoring higher than other district schools. Moreover, our district is consistently one of the top scoring districts in the state. Although we recognize that demographics play a part in the results of standardized testing, we feel confident that we have helped children learn the type of thinking skills that have enabled their success on standardized testing.

Final Thoughts

Our emphasis in assessment was about gathering a body of evidence to showcase children's thinking and document their growth. We looked for children's authentic interaction with text, which we often discovered through discussions and written responses. It was critical to assess the process students used to comprehend text, as well as the product of their thinking. In order to get a true gauge of students' ability to gain meaning, you must know how they arrived at their answers.

Epilogue

During the course of this project of integrating arts and reading comprehension, our district moved our school to another building. Teachers, parents, and students had the opportunity to visit the new site of our school, in a building across town. Elise, a second-grade student, came up to us while she was looking at the building and said, "There's no art anywhere." As we stood in the empty hallway, the teachers made a commitment to create moveable art pieces—unlike the wall murals we had left behind—so we would have something to bring with us to this new school.

Elise's statement made it clear to us that our work with integrating the arts had affected us and the students profoundly. The children had become more aware of the art in the world around them. They also had begun to see themselves as artists and as such, valued their art. For example, when we took a break from our writing one day and went to the farmer's market, we ran into one of our second-grade students. He was thrilled to tell us that he had framed one of his pieces of art and that it was displayed on a table in his living room.

Students also were thriving on the deep level of discussions they were having around books. The fifth-grade girls' book club with whom we were meeting refused to stop meeting, even though they had graduated. They wanted a commitment from us to continue reading and integrating the arts through middle school. Students also developed a great deal of knowledge about the reading comprehension strategies, which they are now proud to rattle off for us at any moment. And they continue to expand on text connections, even inventing new ones such as the text-to-video game connection and the text-to-dream connection. We always are excited when we see children of all ages interacting with text in a sophisticated manner.

Our initial fear—that by using the arts, we would lose the focus of literacy—was unfounded. Rather than detracting from the text, the arts enhanced engagement with it. As teachers, our role was to develop art experiences that would help students focus attention on the author's intent. We also discovered that even when the time and materials were minimal, the students' engagement was extremely high. For instance, using a minute-long tableau instead of an hour-long drama or using a quick sketch instead of a painting was just as effective in keeping students interested in their work. Students' love of the arts as a form of expression energized and focused them.

Further, our work has uncovered for us a new level of understanding about how the arts shape cognition and how that affects comprehension. Watching children light up with a new thought as they are engaged in a drawing or a drama was a delight. The critical connection of visual and kinesthetic learning to thinking has affected our own understanding and teaching of reading comprehension. Using the arts to teach reading comprehension strategies allowed a broader range of students to experience success in reading comprehension. Many students who once struggled with literacy are now able to provide leadership to other students, which gives them a new voice and self-confidence. Children who once responded to invitations to talk about books with a quiet "I don't know" are now spontaneously drawing a picture, writing a poem, or planning a minidrama to express their thinking.

Weaving the arts through the teaching of reading comprehension strategies created a dynamic, compelling curriculum that invited our students into a lifelong relationship with reading. Our program inspired a community of learners to place art at the heart of their learning. We hope that after reading this book, you feel inspired to place art at the heart of your students' learning.

Matrix
of the Arts

e have organized this matrix to help you cross-reference the art forms and reading comprehension strategies in chapters 2–7. For example, if you wanted to use storytelling in the classroom, you would look up *storytelling* in the Art column of the matrix to see which lessons connect this art form to a strategy. In addition to helping classroom teachers, this matrix will assist art specialists to connect art projects to literacy development in the classroom.

156

Art Projects and Drama Techniques

Note: To see images of some completed art projects, refer to specific lessons throughout the chapters.

Art Projects

Clay Pots

Materials
- 25-pound jug of earthenware clay
- decorating tools (fine-pointed tools, forks or spoons, combs, or Popsicle sticks)
- slip (a creamy mixture of clay and water that students can make)

Technique
Start by asking students to roll out 12-inch coils of clay. Remind them to use their fingers to smooth out cracks in the clay. By using slip to add moisture to clay, students should not allow the clay to dry out. To make slip, have students use a small amount of clay and add water, mixing it with their fingers until it has a creamy consistency. Next, students should mark their coils with small markings and cover with slip to help the coils stay together. Have them wrap one coil in a spiral to form a base for the pot, then layer new coils on top of the outer part of the base to raise the sides of the pot. Students should connect the layers by using a fork to make scratch marks, then use the slip to help keep the coils together. During this time, remind students to smooth out any lines with their fingers. Once they finish constructing their pots, students may add decorations gently with fine-pointed tools, forks or spoons, combs, or Popsicle sticks.

Impressionist Tempera Painting for a van Gogh Study

Materials
- pencils
- colored chalk
- tempera paints
- paintbrushes
- tagboard

Technique
This is an simple method of letting children experience the texture of Impressionist artwork such as van Gogh's. Show students how to begin by starting with a pencil outline. Once students have completed their outlines, they may add color by dipping their chosen piece of colored chalk into a dish

of tempera paint of contrasting color. Model how to use short, quick strokes with the chalk, and remind them to dip their chalk into the paint after every third or fourth stroke.

Mask Making

Plaster Masks

Materials
- plaster strips (can be purchased at a pharmacy)
- Vaseline
- acrylic or tempera paint
- paintbrushes
- feathers, glitter, and other objects for decoration

Technique
Note: This project requires that students trust one another. Because some students will not feel comfortable covering their faces in plaster, have premade masks available for them to use.

Be sure to cut the plaster into strips before starting. Then, place students in groups of three or four. Ask one student within each group to volunteer to cover his or her face with Vaseline. After these volunteers have covered their faces, have them lie down so the other students can gently cover their faces with plaster strips that have been wet. Make sure the students do not cover the volunteers' nostrils; students can have their mouths covered but must agree to this beforehand. Once the plaster masks are complete, carefully take them off the students' faces so the masks can dry. Have students decorate dry masks with acrylic paint, feathers, glitter, and other objects.

Milk-Jug Masks

Materials
- one plastic gallon milk jug per student
- newspaper
- liquid starch
- paint and other materials for decoration

Technique
Have students cut the milk jugs in half so that one section has the handle in the center. The students will use papier-mâché on this section of the jug. To

make the papier-mâché, mix the liquid starch with water, making a half-and-half solution. Then, have students help you cut the newspaper into strips. After the cutting is done, students should dip each strip into the liquid solution and place it on the milk-jug mold. Remind students that the strips of paper should not be larger than 1" × 4" and that they should lay them flat on the jug. Once they have covered the whole jug, students should let it dry. Because students can leave the milk jug inside the mask, it is not necessary for them to do a second coat of papier-mâché. When the masks are dry, students can paint and decorate them.

Portrait Painting

Materials
- oil pastels
- watercolor paints
- paintbrushes
- heavy-duty drawing paper or watercolor paper

Technique
Begin by having students use oil pastels to draw their portraits. Model this process for your students, as it is important to help them use the space on the paper. Remind them that white spaces eventually will be the color of their watercolor wash, which allows students to use the paints over the entire portrait. Once their portraits are complete, students may choose a watercolor to wash over the entire portrait. Students are sometimes reluctant to use the wash on the portrait, so you may want to model the finished product of a completed portrait.

Querencias

Materials
- one wood piece 6" × 8" per student
- two wood pieces 3" × 8" per student
- leather scraps
- collage materials, such as paints, beads, buttons, dried flowers, tiny shells and rocks, ribbon, postcards, wrapping paper, and fabric
- magazines (for cutting)
- glue
- scissors

Technique

Give students the opportunity to work on their *querencias* in small groups over a two-day period, allowing an hour and a half of time per day. Students begin by using the leather to attach the two smaller pieces of wood to the larger piece, which creates doors that open with leather hinges. Make a wide range of collage materials available to students, but instruct them to choose the most powerful words and phrases to describe their thinking. After students have cut out materials from magazines to describe their thinking, they should glue these words and phrases to the inside of their *querencias*. Finally, demonstrate how to use other materials as decorative accents.

Quilting

Paper Quilts

Materials
- one piece of butcher paper large enough to accommodate each student's pattern block
- glue
- four 3-inch right triangles in bright colors per student
- one 6-inch square in a contrasting color or pattern per student

Technique

Show children how to fold the squares into four parts and ask them to find as many ways as possible to place the triangles in the squares. Explain to students that there can be only one triangle in each quadrant and that the triangles cannot overlap or go off the edges. After choosing an arrangement, students may glue their triangles on the square and place it on a larger piece of paper to make the quilt.

Fabric Quilts

Materials
- scissors
- backing fabric that is slightly larger than the finished quilt top
- batting for the middle of the quilt
- 2.5-inch fabric strips for borders between squares (number of strips needed will depend on the number of squares)
- four 3-inch right triangles in bright colors per student
- one 6-inch square of fabric in a contrasting color or pattern per student

- one needle and thread per student
- four 3-inch right triangles of fabric adhesive per student

Technique

Students should copy their favorite paper square pattern in fabric or create a new pattern if this is the first time they are participating in a quilting project. Using a fabric adhesive, students can then attach the triangles to the squares before sewing the squares to the quilt. A parent or other volunteer should sew together the squares with a 2-inch border between the squares. When the quilt top, batting, and backing are put together, students may complete the actual hand quilting during read-aloud time throughout the year, or they can hand tie it for a quick finish.

Sand Tray Worlds

Materials
- four pieces of wood 3" × 24"
- one piece of flat board 24" × 24"
- screws and a drill
- fine sand
- small figures of animals, people, and imaginary characters
- small natural objects, such as shells, driftwood, jewels or stones, nuts, and pine cones

Technique

Use the wood and flat board to build a 24-inch square tray for the sand. This tray will be the workspace in which students build their miniature worlds. The more figures and natural objects you are able to collect, the more enticing this area will become for students. (You may want to keep the area organized by using baskets to sort figures of animals and people and natural objects. It also may be helpful to keep a broom and dustpan available for children to clean up sand when they are finished.) Once students have completed their sand-tray worlds, use a digital camera to record the worlds. Students can then use these photographs when writing stories about their worlds or when writing in their reading-response logs.

Shadow-Puppet Theater

Materials
- overhead projector and colored transparencies

- a white bedsheet
- dark fabric
- thick black construction paper or tagboard
- dowels
- coarse materials, such as small dried flowers and plants, and other objects for decoration
- clear Plexiglas dish
- food coloring

Technique

Theater and Background

Use the white sheet as the top part of the theater, and attach the dark fabric to the bottom of the sheet. You can either sew the material together, or use pins to hold it together. Then, hang the sheet from the ceiling with at least 10 feet behind it for the overhead projector and the student performers. Place the overhead projector on a desk behind the sheet.

For the theater's background, ask students to draw mountain ranges or forest scenes, then copy them onto transparencies. After students have completed these larger elements of the background, have them cut out designs to add details such as a large tree or a farmhouse. These details can be placed on top of the background transparency. For backgrounds, you also can photocopy old black-and-white pictures onto transparencies. When students have completed the backgrounds, place the backgrounds on the overhead projector.

Effects

Students may use special effects to add the illusion of a colorful sky or moving water. To show changes in the sky, students hold colored transparencies in front of the projector lightbulb. By slowly moving the colored transparencies back and forth, students can give the illusion of dawn or dusk. If students want to show moving water, have them fill a clear dish with water, add different colors and objects to the water, and hold it over the background. When they gently move and swirl the dish, students can create different water effects on the screen.

Puppets

Begin by asking students to make a sketches of the characters on paper. A puppet of a human should be 4–5 inches tall; everything else within the play should be in proportion to the puppet playing the main character. It is best if students sketch profiles of their characters. Once they finish their sketches, have students copy their characters onto thick black construction paper or tagboard. After copying the pictures, students should cut out the characters and attach the paper to the top of 2–3-foot dowels. Some students may want to show unique details of their puppets, such as flames shooting out of a dragon's mouth or bags being held. These details can be added using transparencies, material, and dried flowers.

When the puppets are ready for the show, have the performers kneel down behind the dark part of the screen and hold the puppets so their shadows are projected against the white sheet. Tell students that the puppets should be right next to the sheet but not resting on it. Smaller movements by the puppets tend to be more effective; for special movements, students should twirl and spin the puppets.

Sock Dolls

Materials
- one pair of socks per student
- stuffing
- needles and thread
- string, yarn, or ribbon
- buttons, glitter, shells, embroidery thread, and other materials for decoration (children also can bring in items from home)

Technique
Have student use a pair of socks for each doll. Begin by having them cut the top 3 inches off one sock, leaving them with a 3-inch wide sock band. Students should then cut the band lengthwise, leaving them with two rectangles. These rectangles will become the doll's arms. Next, students will begin making the doll's body and legs. Using the second sock, students should cut from the top of the sock to the heel. The heel of the sock becomes the bottom of the doll, and there should be two distinct legs.

Next, have students start sewing. They should begin by sewing up the inside legs, then the arms. Make sure students leave enough space in these areas so they can add stuffing to the doll. Once the body and legs are stuffed, have students sew up the holes completely. Then, students take a piece of string, yarn, or ribbon to make the doll's neck. Have them tie the string around the neck about 2 inches down from the sock's toe. Students should wrap the ribbon around the neck a couple of times and pull it tight to create the doll's head. Then, ask students to attach the arms to the doll's body below the neck. The doll's body should now be complete.

Finally, students may use yarn, buttons, material, glitter, shells, embroidery thread, and other decorations to bring their dolls to life.

Wet-on-Wet Watercolor Painting

Materials
• heavy stock paper or watercolor paper
• watercolor paints (premixed wet paints or watercolor sets)
• sponges
• brushes
• jars for water

Technique
Have students help pass out all the materials so they are ready when it is time to begin. Once students have all the materials, have them watch you as you model painting in the wet-on-wet style. Begin by using a sponge to make the whole piece of paper wet. Then using a brush, start painting with the lightest color, and slowly add the darker colors (it is best to limit the color choice to three or four colors). Remind students that the colors will run together and that this a unique aspect of this style of painting.

When you have finished painting the paper, try some other interesting techniques such as:

- sprinkling salt on the picture to make it look like it is snowing,
- using the back of the paintbrush as a pencil to add lines or patterns, or
- using a dry paintbrush to brush off some of the wet paint and make the area lighter.

Once you have showed students these techniques, they may begin to paint.

Drama Techniques

The drama techniques used in this book include process drama, tableau, and dramatic interview. In order for these techniques to be effective, you need to model the authenticity of being in role. One aspect of creating excellent drama

167

experiences is holding high expectations for students' abilities to be in role. Often when students begin drama, their natural response is to be silly. By responding to their actions in role, you may be able to set the standard for the drama and help them overcome their awkwardness.

Another issue often encountered with these drama techniques is that students may not have the background knowledge to be authentic in their roles. When this happens, you may choose to stop the drama and use this as a teaching moment. Make sure students know you are no longer in role. Ask the rest of the class to share information pertaining to the issue. After students have had a chance to share, resume the drama where you left off. This teaching moment gives students a second chance at integrating new knowledge into their roles.

Process Drama

This style of drama is embedded into your curriculum and does not focus on the actual drama performance. Process dramas tend to be very short and to the point. Students become characters from text and in their roles as characters, seek to resolve or gain a better understanding of problems or tensions in the text.

Begin by choosing a scene from the text or creating a scene that is an extension of one from the text. Choose scenes that are open-ended and allow for many interpretations or that may provide a poignant experience for students. Then, assign characters to students and introduce the scene through discussion or through the arrival of a letter that you have created (although you may choose to include props, they are not necessary). Ask students to create their own dialogue and movement in response to the situation presented. After the drama, have students discuss the scene or respond in writing in their journals.

Tableau

A tableau is a frozen frame or photo from a scene. It focuses on one idea, event, or even a word. Start by having students create an image using their bodies. Tell them to focus on gesture, composition, facial expression, and the overall message they want to send the viewer. Explain that gesture helps viewers create inferences by the way characters place their bodies and that composition focuses on the relationship between the different people in the scene. One element of composition that creates a dynamic tableau is the use of several different heights between characters.

Once students have created their scene, have them hold it for two minutes while you and the students question and critique the image. As the teacher, feel comfortable asking students to try variations of the scene to elicit further questions and responses from students.

Dramatic Interview

This drama technique requires that students become characters from the text and may involve one character or a panel of characters in an interview. These students may wear name tags with characters' names on them to help other students differentiate the character from the student. You may be either a moderator, as in a debate, or a participant. Instruct students in the audience to ask the characters questions that relate to the text (students may ask as many questions as they want). You may want to begin by modeling the types of questions that will help students learn more about the text's deeper meaning, thus encouraging them to ask similar questions. Remind students who are playing characters that they will need to rely on their use of the reading comprehension strategies in order to answer the questions from the character's point of view. If you are interested in assessing students' thinking through a written response, have them write their inferences in a double-entry journal before and after the interview.

Blackline Masters of Assessment Forms

Arts Observation Guide for Construction

Name: _____

Date: _____

Art-Based Activity: _____

Comprehension Strategy: _____

Evidence of Arts Elements	Arts Elements	Evidence of Meaning Making
	Balance Uses symmetry or asymmetry in design	
	Structure Demonstrates strength, quality, and technique and matches function	
	Design Shows line, shape, repetition, contrast, variation, and texture	
	Material Choices Uses materials appropriate to purpose	
	Decorative Elements Uses elements that are innovative, appealing, and symbolic	

Observations and comments:

Arts Observation Guide for Dance and Movement

Name: _____

Date: _____

Art-Based Activity: _____

Comprehension Strategy: _____

Evidence of Arts Elements	Arts Elements	Evidence of Meaning Making
	Body Communicates, controls, and expresses rhythms and tempo	
	Energy Demonstrates strong flow, appropriate energy, and mood	
	Communication Problem solves and uses symbolism	
	Choreography Improvises and shows variety in use of space, levels, and shapes	
	Focus Concentrates, shows engagement, and follows directions	

Observations and comments:

Arts Observation Guide for Drama

Name: _____

Date: _____

Art-Based Activity: _____

Comprehension Strategy: _____

Evidence of Arts Elements	Arts Elements	Evidence of Meaning Making
	Voice Is fluent, clear, and expressive	
	Character Is believable, stays in role, and develops character's point of view	
	Improvisation Is flexible, spontaneous, and reflective, elaborates on ideas, and problem solves	
	Movement Shows good use of energy and control of actions and communicates with gestures	
	Focus Shows engagement, concentrates, and explores questions	

Observations and comments:

Arts Observation Guide for Music

Name: _____

Date: _____

Art-Based Activity: _____

Comprehension Strategy: _____

Evidence of Arts Elements	Arts Elements	Evidence of Meaning Making
	Responds to Music Builds preferences, knows terminology, and responds with purposeful movement	
	Creates Music Knows genres, responds in same style, embellishes, and creates variations	
	Performs With Instruments Demonstrates pattern, rhythm, and tempo	
	Sings Uses expression, is responsive to conductor, and knows genres	

Observations and comments:

Arts Observation Guide for Visual Arts

Name: _____

Date: _____

Art-Based Activity: _____

Comprehension Strategy:_____

Evidence of Arts Elements	Arts Elements	Evidence of Meaning Making
	Composition Arranges elements in a certain way	
	Color Deliberates about color choice, shading, and use of light	
	Line and Shape Shows strength, movement, pattern, and feeling or action	
	Mood Demonstrates a feeling and a message	
	Perspective Uses background, foreground, and middle ground	

Observations and comments:

Book Club Response—Artful Artist

Name: _____

Book: _____

Assignment: page _____ to page _____

Directions: Draw anything about the story you like (a character, the setting, a problem, an exciting part, a surprise, or a prediction) on this piece of paper or another piece. When you meet with your group, let them guess and talk about the drawing first, and then you can share.

Source: Adapted from the Boulder Valley School District Literacy Journey Handbook.

Book Club Response–Connector

Name: _____

Book: _____

Assignment: page _____ to page _____

Directions: Find connections in the book you are reading. Often, these connections are to your life, other books you have read, or the world. While reading, find five connections to share with your group. Write down the page number and what the connection was.

1. Page _____

Connection: _____

_____

_____

2. Page _____

Connection: _____

_____

_____

3. Page _____

Connection: _____

_____

_____

4. Page _____

Connection: _____

_____

_____

5. Page _____

Connection: _____

_____

_____

Source: Adapted from the Boulder Valley School District Literacy Journey Handbook.

Book Club Response–Discussion Director

Name: _____

Book: _____

Assignment: page _____ to page _____

Directions: Come up with three or four questions that you would like to discuss with the group. Often, the best questions are open-ended and do not have one right or wrong answer.

Questions that I want to share with the group today:

1. _____

   _____

2. _____

   _____

3. _____

   _____

4. _____

   _____

Source: Adapted from the Boulder Valley School District Literacy Journey Handbook.

Book Club Response—Investigator

Name: _____

Book: _____

Assignment: page _____ to page _____

Directions: In the section you are reading, find words or phrases whose meaning is unclear to you or that you thought were interesting or wonderful. Write down six of these words, and either investigate to find out the meaning of each word or explain why you think it is interesting.

1._____ on page _____
Definition or why it is interesting:

_____

_____

2. _____ on page _____
Definition or why it is interesting:

_____

_____

3._____ on page _____
Definition or why it is interesting:

_____

_____

4._____ on page _____
Definition or why it is interesting:

_____

_____

5._____ on page _____
Definition or why it is interesting:

_____

_____

6._____ on page _____
Definition or why it is interesting:

_____

_____

Source: Adapted from the Boulder Valley School District Literacy Journey Handbook.

Weaving Through Words: Using the Arts to Teach Reading Comprehension Strategies by Roberta D. Mantione and Sabine Smead ©2003. Newark, DE: International Reading Association. May be copied for classroom use.

Book Club Response—Literary Luminary

Name: _____

Book: _____

Assignment: page _____ to page _____

Directions: Select four funny, puzzling, powerful, or important passages from the book you are reading. Then, write down why you chose each passage and how you would like to share it.

1. Passage starts on page _____.
The first word is _____. The last word is _____.
Reason: _____
_____
Plan for sharing: _____

2. Passage starts on page _____.
The first word is _____. The last word is _____.
Reason: _____
_____
Plan for sharing: _____

3. Passage starts on page _____.
The first word is _____. The last word is _____.
Reason: _____
_____
Plan for sharing: _____

4. Passage starts on page _____.
The first word is _____. The last word is _____.
Reason: _____
_____
Plan for sharing: _____

Source: Adapted from the Boulder Valley School District Literacy Journey Handbook.

Weaving Through Words: Using the Arts to Teach Reading Comprehension Strategies by Roberta D. Mantione and Sabine Smead ©2003. Newark, DE: International Reading Association. May be copied for classroom use.

Book Club Response—Travel Tracer

Name: _____

Book: _____

Assignment: page _____ to page _____

Directions: Often, it is important to know where things are happening in order to understand the story and to keep track of the plot, the events, and the setting in the story. While you read, keep track of the major events, as well as the description of the setting. Make sure you write down the page number of the description.

The action begins at _____   Page on which it is described _____
(describe setting)

_____

_____

_____

_____

_____

_____

The major events took place at _____   Page on which it is described _____
(describe major events)

_____

_____

_____

_____

_____

_____

This section of events ends at _____   Page on which it is described _____

_____

_____

_____

_____

_____

_____

Source: Adapted from the Boulder Valley School District Literacy Journey Handbook.

Weaving Through Words: Using the Arts to Teach Reading Comprehension Strategies by Roberta D. Mantione and Sabine Smead ©2003. Newark, DE: International Reading Association. May be copied for classroom use.

Double-Entry Journal

Name:_____   **Date:**_____

On this side, copy a short meaningful quote or details from the text or poem.	On this side, use the reading comprehension strategy of _____ to comment on the text.

Observation Checklist to Look for Evidence of Growth in Comprehension

Name:_____   Date:_____

Book Title:_____

Art Project: (circle one) Whole-class discussion   Small-group discussion
                              Reading-response log   Art activity

<u>**Strategy**</u>   <u>**Evidence From Child's Response**</u>

Developing Sensory Images
- Makes pictures in mind
- Uses multiple senses
- Includes an emotional component
- Adds detail through imagery
- Develops a mental model to organize meaning

Building and Activating Schema
- Makes text-to-self connections
- Makes text-to-text connections
- Makes text-to-world connections
- Uses connections to build meaning

Questioning
- Asks yes or no questions
- Asks higher level questions
- Asks questions to clarify author's intent
- Uses questioning to evolve in his or her thinking

Determining Importance
- Distinguishes between details and essential ideas
- Recognizes important themes

Inferring
- Communicates emotional content of text
- Has insight into the characters and events of story
- Makes predictions based on inferences of text
- Creates a personal interpretation
- Discovers author's implied messages

Synthesis
- Creates a summary of the text
- Discovers commonalities in texts
- Generates new meaning based on author's ideas and own personal interpretations

183

Reading-Response Log

Name: _____

Title: _____

Directions: Write down your response, or what the reading made you think, feel, or wonder. Then, write a short summary of the reading.

Response

_____
_____
_____
_____
_____
_____
_____
_____
_____
_____
_____
_____

Summary

_____
_____
_____
_____
_____
_____
_____
_____
_____
_____
_____
_____

Art and Literacy Resources

Books That Support Integration of the Arts

A'Court, A., Jackson, P., & Elliot, M. (2000). *The art and craft of paper*. London: Southwater.

Berensohn, P. (1972). *Finding one's way with clay: Creating pinched pottery and working with colored clays*. New York: Simon & Schuster.

Blecher, S., & Jaffee, K. (1998). *Weaving in the arts: Widening the learning circle*. Portsmouth, NH: Heinemann.

Brooke, S. (1998). *Hooked on painting: Illustrated lessons & exercises for grades 4 and up*. Paramus, NJ: Prentice Hall.

Chancer, J., & Rester-Zodrow, G. (1997). *Moon journals: Writing, art, and inquiry through focused nature study*. Portsmouth, NH: Heinemann.

Cheek, M. (2002). *Design sourcebook: Mosaics*. London: New Holland.

Chertok, B., Hirshfeld, G., & Rosh, M. (1993). *Learning about ancient civilizations through art*. New York: Scholastic.

Dobbs, S.M. (1998). *Learning in and through art: A guide to discipline-based art education*. Los Angeles: Getty Education Institute for the Arts.

England, K., & Johnson, M.E. (2000). *Quilt inspirations from Africa: A caravan of ideas, patterns, motifs, and techniques*. Lincolnwood, IL: Quilt Digest Press.

Fowler, C.B. (1996). *Strong arts, strong schools: The promising potential and shortsighted disregard of the arts in American schooling*. New York: Oxford University Press.

Gardner, H. (1990). *Art education and human development*. Los Angeles: Getty Center for Education in the Arts.

Gourley, M. (2001). *Cloth dolls: How to make them* (Rev. ed.). Lincolnwood, IL: Quilt Digest Press/NTC Publishing Group.

Hamilton, M., & Weiss, M. (1990). *Children tell stories: A teaching guide*. Katonah, NY: Richard C. Owen.

Haslam, A., & Glover, D. (1994). *Building*. Ill. J. Barnes. New York: Thomson Learning.

Heard, G. (1989). *For the good of Earth and sun: Teaching poetry*. Portsmouth, NH: Heinemann.

Hucko, B. (1996). *Where there is no name for art: The art of Tewa pueblo children*. Santa Fe, NM: School of American Research.

Jensen, E. (2001). *Arts with the brain in mind*. Alexandria, VA: Association for Supervision and Curriculum Development.

Kong, E. (1999). *The great clay adventure: Creative handbuilding for young artists*. Worcester, MA: Davis.

Leslie, C.W., & Roth, C.E. (1998). *Nature journaling: Learning to observe and connect with the world around you*. Pownal, VT: Storey Books.

Leslie, C.W., & Roth, C.E. (2000). *Keeping a nature journal: Discover a whole new way of seeing the world around you*. Pownal, VT: Storey Books.

Livo, N.J., & Rietz, S.A. (1986). *Storytelling: Process and practice*. Englewood, CO: Libraries Unlimited.

Livo, N.J., & Rietz, S.A. (1991). *Storytelling: Folklore sourcebook*. Englewood, CO: Libraries Unlimited.

London, P. (1994). *Step outside: Community-based art education*. Portsmouth, NH: Heinemann.

Lyons, M.E. (1993). *Stitching stars: The story quilts of Harriet Powers*. New York: Atheneum.

MacDonald, M.R. (2000). *Shake-it-up tales! Stories to sing, dance, drum, and act out*. Little Rock, AR: August House.

Rubright, L. (1996). *Beyond the beanstalk: Interdisciplinary learning through storytelling*. Portsmouth, NH: Heinemann.

Smith-Autard, J.M. (2002). *The art of dance in education* (2nd ed.). London: A. & C. Black.

Wates, R. (2000). *The mosaic idea book: More than 100 designs to copy and create*. Cincinnati, OH: North Light Books.

White, K., & Parker, C. (2000). *Papier mâché*. Marlborough, UK: Crowood.

Websites

AllPosters.com
http://www.allposters.com

Art Network: Museums
http://www.art4net.com/ARTMUSEUMS+.html

Association for the Advancement of Arts Education (AAAE)
http://aaae.org

Blue Heron Dolls: Storybook Doll
http://www.blueherondolls.com/storybook_doll.htm

Crayola Creativity Central
http://www.crayola.com

Creative Drama and Theatre Education Resource Site
http://www.creativedrama.com

Eyes on Art
http://www.kn.pacbell.com/wired/art2/index.html

Florida Art Education Association (FAEA)
http://www.faea.org

Getty Arts Ed Net
http://www.getty.edu/artsednet

Harvard Graduate School of Education Arts in Education Homepage
http://www.gse.harvard.edu/~aie_web

Harvard Project Zero
http://pzweb.harvard.edu

International Reading Association: *The Reading Teacher*
http://www.reading.org/publications/rt/index.html

The Kennedy Center: ArtsEdge
http://artsedge.kennedy-center.org

Kinder Art/Art Lessons
http://www.kinderart.com/index.html

Kodak: Education—Art: Lesson Plans
http://www.Kodak.com/global/en/consumer/education/lessonPlans/indices/art.shtml

The Learning Page: Lesson Plans
http://memory.loc.gov/ammem/ndlpedu/lessons

London Association of Art and Design Education
http://www.laade.org

Michael C. Carlos Museum/Permanent Collection: Sub-Saharan African Art
http://carlos.emory.edu/COLLECTION/AFRICA

The Morgan Library
http://www.morganlibrary.org

Museum Tours
http://www.museum-tours.com

National Art Education Association (NAEA)
http://www.naea-reston.org

National Endowment for the Arts
http://www.nea.gov

National Gallery/London: Tell Us a Picture
http://nationalgallery.org.uk/education/tellus/01story.htm

Perpich Center for Arts Education
http://www.mcae.k12.mn.us

Storyteller.net
http://www.storyteller.net

Storytelling, Drama, Creative Dramatics, Puppetry, & Readers Theater for Children & Young Adults
http://falcon.jmu.edu/~ramseyil/drama.htm

Theatre Lesson Plan Exchange
http://www.geocities.com/shalyndria13

UNSW COFA School of Art Education
http://www.arted.cofa.unsw.edu.au

The Vincent van Gogh Gallery
http://www.vangoghgallery.com

Vincent van Gogh Museum
http://www.vangoghmuseum.nl

Vincent van Gogh Paintings Project
http://home.wanadoo.nl/vincentvangogh

Virtual Curriculum: Elementary Art Education
http://www.dhc.net/~artgeek/index.html

Weir Dolls: Index of Supplies
http://www.weirdolls.com/supplies

Wits End Mosaic
http://www.mosaic-witsend.com

The World of Puppets
http://www.itdc.sbcss.k12.ca.us/curriculum/puppetry.html

Art Suppliers

Chinaberry, Inc.—resource for carefully selected books, tapes, and crafts
2780 Via Orange Way, Suite B
Spring Valley, CA 91978
Phone: 800-776-2242
Website: http://www.chinaberry.com

Dharma Trading Co.—resource for reasonably priced cotton and silk materials, dyes, and batik kits
PO Box 150916
San Rafael, CA 94915
Phone: 800-542-5227
Website: http://www.dharmatrading.com

Dick Blick Art Materials—resource for reasonably priced art supplies
PO Box 1267
Galesburg, IL 61402
Phone: 800-828-4548
Website: http://www.dickblick.com

Earthsong Fibers—resource for weaving, spinning, felting, and dyeing supplies and books
5115 Excelsior Boulevard, No. 428
Minneapolis, MN 55416
Phone: 800-473-5350
Website: http://www.earthsongfibers.com

Laguna Clay Company—resource for clay tools and materials
14400 Lomitas Avenue
City of Industry, CA 91746
Phone: 800-452-4862
Website: http://www.lagunaclay.com

Paper, Scissors, Stone—resource for high quality watercolors, colored pencils, and sketchbooks and journals
PO Box 428
Viroqua, WI 54665
Phone: 888-644-5843
Website: http://www.waldorfsupplies.com/frames/frameset.html

References

Andrews, R. (1993). *The Columbia dictionary of quotations*. New York: Columbia University Press.

Bang, M. (2000). *Picture this: How pictures work*. New York: SeaStar Books.

Bell, N. (1991). *Visualizing and verbalizing: For language comprehension and thinking*. San Luis Obispo, CA: Gander Educational Publishing.

Boutan, M. (1996). *Matisse: Art activity pack*. San Francisco: Chronicle Books.

Boutan, M. (1998). *Picasso: Art activity pack*. San Francisco: Chronicle Books.

Bransford, J.D., Brown, A.L., & Cocking, R.R. (Eds.). (2000). *How people learn: Brain, mind, experience, and school*. Washington, DC: National Academy Press.

Burmark, L. (2002). *Visual literacy: Learn to see, see to learn*. Alexandria, VA: Association for Supervision and Curriculum Development.

Burton, J., Horowitz, R., & Abeles, H. (2000). Learning in and through the arts: Curriculum implications. In E.B. Fiske (Ed.), *Champions of change: The impact of the arts on learning* (pp. 36–46). Retrieved November 20, 2000, from http://artsedge. kennedy-center.org/champions

Cameron, J. (1992). *The artist's way: A spiritual path to higher creativity*. New York: Putnam.

Catterall, J.S., Chapleau, R., & Iwanaga, J. (2000). Involvement in the arts and human development: General involvement and intensive involvement in music and theater arts. In E.B. Fiske (Ed.), *Champions of change: The impact of the arts on learning* (pp. 2–18). Retrieved November 20, 2000, from http://artsedge.kennedy-center.org/champions

Cecil, N.L., & Lauritzen, P. (1994). *Literacy and the arts for the integrated classroom: Alternative ways of knowing*. White Plains, NY: Longman.

Cornett, C.E. (1998). *The arts as meaning makers: Integrating literature and the arts throughout the curriculum*. Upper Saddle River, NJ: Prentice Hall.

Eisner, E.W. (1994). *Cognition and curriculum reconsidered* (2nd ed.). New York: Teachers College Press.

Emmitt, M. (1998, August). Are we overselling literacy? Connections between arts and literacy learning in school. Paper presented at the Cross Arts Seminar in South Yarra, Victoria, Australia. Retrieved March 3, 2002, from http://www.netspace.net.au/~xav/seminars/seminar3_98/are_we_overselling_literac.htm

Fritz, J. (1992). *Surprising myself*. Katonah, NY: Richard C. Owen.

Gardner, H. (1983). *Frames of mind: The theory of multiple intelligences*. New York: Basic Books.

Harvey, S., & Goudvis, A. (2000). *Strategies that work: Teaching comprehension to enhance understanding*. York, ME: Stenhouse.

Heathcote, D., & Bolton, G.M. (1995). *Drama for learning: Dorothy Heathcote's mantle of the expert approach to education*. Portsmouth, NH: Heinemann.

Jensen, E. (2001). *Arts with the brain in mind*. Alexandria, VA: Association for Supervision and Curriculum Development.

Keene, E.O., & Zimmermann, S. (1997). *Mosaic of thought: Teaching comprehension in a reader's workshop*. Portsmouth, NH: Heinemann.

Kohn, A. (2000). *The case against standardized testing: Raising the scores, ruining the schools*. Portsmouth, NH: Heinemann.

Long, S.A., Winograd, P.N., & Bridge, C.A. (1989). The effects of reader and text characteristics on reports of imagery during and after reading. *Reading Research Quarterly, 24*, 353–372.

McKeown, M.G., & Beck, I.L. (2001). Designing questions toward thinking and understanding rather than answers. *Perspectives, 27*(2), 21–24.

McMann, J. (1998). *Altars and icons: Sacred spaces in everyday life*. San Francisco: Chronicle Books.

Miller, D. (2002). *Reading with meaning: Teaching comprehension in the primary grades*. York, ME: Stenhouse.

Perkins, D.N. (1994). *The intelligent eye: Learning to think by looking at art*. Los Angeles: Getty Education Institute for the Arts.

Perkins, D.N. (1995). *Smart schools: Better thinking and learning for every child*. New York: Free Press.

Wagner, B.J. (1998). *Educational drama and language arts: What research shows*. Portsmouth, NH: Heinemann.

Wilhelm, J.D., & Edmiston, B. (1998). *Imaging to learn: Inquiry, ethics, and integration through drama*. Portsmouth, NH: Heinemann.

Wooldridge, S.G. (1996) *Poemcrazy: Freeing your life with words*. New York: Three Rivers Press.

Literature Cited

Agee, J. (1988). *The incredible painting of Felix Clousseau*. New York: Farrar, Straus & Giroux.

Ancona, G. (1993). *Pablo remembers: The fiesta of the Day of the Dead*. New York: Lothrop, Lee & Shepard.

Aristotle. (1972). *Aristotle on memory* (R. Sorabji, Trans.). Providence, RI: Brown University Press.

Barrett, T. (1999). *Anna of Byzantium*. New York: Delacorte.

Baylor, B. (1972). *When clay sings*. Ill. T. Bahti. New York: Scribner.

Brown, M.W. (1949). *The important book*. Ill. L. Weisgard. New York: Harper.

Bunting, E. (1990). *How many days to America: A Thanksgiving story*. Ill. B. Peck. Boston: Houghton Mifflin.

Buss, F.L. (with Cubias, D.). (1993). *Journey of the sparrows*. New York: Dell.

Collier, B. (2000). *Uptown*. New York: Henry Holt.

Coville, B. (Retell.). (1996). *William Shakespeare's* A Midsummer Night's Dream. Ill. D. Nolan. New York: Dial.

Doubilet, A. (1991). *Under the sea from A to Z.* Photo. D. Doubilet. New York: Crown.

Cushman, K. (1994). *Catherine, called Birdy.* New York: Clarion Books.

Cushman, K. (1996). *The ballad of Lucy Whipple.* New York: Clarion Books.

Demi. (1998). *The Dalai Lama: A biography of the Tibetan spiritual and political leader.* New York: Henry Holt.

dePaola, T. (1983). *The legend of the bluebonnet: An old tale of Texas.* New York: G.P. Putnam's Sons.

DeSpain, P. (1998). *The dancing turtle: A folktale from Brazil.* Ill. D. Boston. Little Rock, AR: August House.

Dionetti, M. (1996). *Painting the wind: A story of Vincent Van Gogh.* Ill. K. Hawkes. Boston: Little, Brown.

Dunham, M. (1998). *John Muir, young naturalist.* Ill. A. Fiorentino. New York: Aladdin. (Original work published 1975)

Filipovic, Z. (1994). *Zlata's diary: A child's life in Sarajevo.* New York: Viking.

Fitzhugh, L. (1964). *Harriet the spy.* New York: Dell Yearling.

Fleischman, P. (1997). *Seedfolks.* New York: HarperCollins.

Forsyth, A. (1988). *Journey through a tropical jungle.* New York: Simon & Schuster.

George, K.O. (1998a). Tree horse. In *Old Elm speaks: Tree poems* (p. 21). Ill. K. Kiesler. New York: Clarion Books.

George, K.O. (1998b). Tree's place. In *Old Elm speaks: Tree poems* (p. 25). Ill. K. Kiesler. New York: Clarion Books.

Gheerbrant, A. (1992). *The Amazon: Past, present, and future.* New York: Abrams. (Original work published 1988)

Gresko, M.S. (1997). *Roberto Clemente.* Huntington Beach, CA: Teacher Created Materials.

Heide, F.P., & Gilliland, J.H. (1999). *The house of wisdom.* Ill. M. GrandPré. New York: Dorling Kindersley.

Hesse, K. (1997). *Out of the dust.* New York: Scholastic.

Hughes, L. (1994a). Long trip. In *The Dream Keeper and other poems* (p. 16). Ill. B. Pinkney. New York: Knopf.

Hughes, L. (1994b). Poem. In *The Dream Keeper and other poems* (p. 12). Ill. B. Pinkney. New York: Knopf.

Isom, J.S. (1997). *The first starry night.* Dallas, TX: Whispering Coyote Press.

James, J.A. (1999). *The drums of Noto Hanto.* Ill. Tsukushi. New York: Dorling Kindersley.

Johnston, T. (1996). Poor. In *Once in the country: Poems of a farm* (p. 28). Ill. T.B. Allen. New York: Putnam.

Joosse, B.M. (2001). *Ghost wings.* Ill. G. Potter. San Francisco: Chronicle Books.

Katz, B. (2000). *We the people.* Ill. N. Crews. New York: Greenwillow Books.

Kren, T. (1997). *Masterpieces of the J. Paul Getty Museum: Illuminated manuscripts.* Los Angeles: The J. Paul Getty Museum.

Lawrence, J. (1993). *The great migration: An American story.* New York: Museum of Modern Art; Washington, DC: Phillips Collection; New York: HarperCollins.

Levine, G.C. (1999). *Dave at night*. New York: HarperCollins.

London, J. (1996). *Hip cat*. Ill. W. Hubbard. San Francisco: Chronicle Books.

Lourie, P. (1991). *Amazon: A young reader's look at the last frontier*. Photo. M. Santilli. Honesdale, PA: Boyds Mills Press.

Love, D.A. (1995). *Bess's log cabin quilt*. Ill. R. Himler. New York: Holiday House.

Lowery, L. (1999). *Aunt Clara Brown: Official pioneer*. Ill. J.L. Porter. Minneapolis: Carolrhoda.

Lowry, L. (1989). *Number the stars*. New York: Dell.

Lynch, A. (1996) *Great buildings*. Alexandria, VA: Time-Life Books.

MacDonald, M.R. (1992). *Peace tales: World folktales to talk about*. Hamden, CT: Linnet Books.

MacLachlan, P. (1985). *Sarah, plain and tall*. New York: Harper & Row.

Mann, E. (1996). *The Brooklyn Bridge*. Ill. A. Witschonke. New York: Mikaya Press.

Mason, A. (1995). *Matisse: An introduction to the artist's life and work*. Hauppauge, NY: Barron's Educational Series.

Mazer, A. (1991). *The salamander room*. Ill. S. Johnson. New York: Knopf.

McDermott, G. (1980). *Papagayo, the mischief maker*. New York: Windmill/Wanderer.

McGill, A. (2000). *In the hollow of your hand: Slave lullabies*. Ill. M. Cummings. Boston: Houghton Mifflin.

McGovern, A. (1992). *...If you lived in colonial times*. Ill. J. Otani. New York: Scholastic.

McSwigan, M. (1942). *Snow treasure*. New York: E.P. Dutton.

Monceaux, M. (Ill.), & Katcher, R. (1999). *My heroes, my people: African Americans and Native Americans in the West*. New York: Francis Foster Books.

Morris, N. (2000). *Ancient Egypt*. Ill. P. Ravaglia. New York: Peter Bedrick Books.

Myers, C. (2000). *Wings*. New York: Scholastic.

Myers, W.D. (1997). *Harlem: A poem*. Ill. C. Myers. New York: Scholastic.

Nye, N.S. (1999). *What have you lost?* New York: Greenwillow Books.

Oliver, M. (1992). The summer day. In *New and selected poems* (p. 94). Boston: Beacon Press.

Paterson, K. (1999). *The king's equal*. Ill. C. Woodbridge. New York: Harper Trophy.

Patterson, A. (1992). *A field guide to rock art symbols of the greater Southwest*. Boulder, CO: Johnson Books.

Pinkney, A.D. (1998). *Duke Ellington: The piano prince and his orchestra*. Ill. B. Pinkney. New York: Hyperion.

Snape, J., & Snape, C. (1991). *Frog odyssey*. New York: MacRae.

Speare, E.G. (1958). *The witch of Blackbird Pond*. New York: Houghton Mifflin.

Stanley, J. (1992). *Children of the Dust Bowl: The true story of the school at Weedpatch Camp*. New York: Crown.

Stewart, S. (2001). *The journey*. Ill. D. Small. New York: Farrar, Straus & Giroux.

Taylor, H.P. (2000). *Secrets of the stone*. New York: Farrar, Straus & Giroux.

Taylor, T. (1969). *The cay*. Garden City, NY: Doubleday.

Tobin, J., & Dobard, R.G. (1999). *Hidden in plain view: A secret story of quilts and the Underground Railroad*. New York: Doubleday.

van Gogh, V. (1888). Personal letter. Retrieved January 17, 2000, from http://www.van
 goghgallery.com/letters/to_theo_arles.htm

Walker, A. (2001). Women. In B. Rochelle (Sel.), *Words with wings: A treasury of African-
 American poetry and art* (n.p.). New York: HarperCollins/Amistad.

Weeks, S. (1994). *Crocodile smile: 10 songs of the Earth as the animals see it.* Ill. L. Ehlert.
 New York: HarperCollins.

White, E.B. (1970). *The trumpet of the swan.* Ill. F. Marcellino. New York: HarperCollins.

Wilson, B.K. (Retell.). (1993). *Wishbones: A folk tale from China.* Ill. M. So. New York:
 Bradbury Press; Toronto: Maxwell Macmillan Canada; New York: Maxwell
 Macmillan International.

Winter, J. (1988). *Follow the drinking gourd.* New York: Knopf.

Zwinger, S. (1999). *The last wild edge: One woman's journey from the Arctic Circle to the
 Olympic rain forest.* Boulder, CO: Johnson Books.

Artwork and Music Cited

Cassatt, M. (1881). *Woman and child driving* [Oil on canvas]. Philadelphia Museum of Art.

Ellington, D. (1931). Mood indigo. On *Ellington at Newport 1956* [Double CD]. New York:
 Sony Music Entertainment. (1999)

Ellington, D., & Strayhorn, B. (1939). Take the "A" train [Recorded by D. Ellington]. On
 Ellington at Newport 1956 [Double CD]. New York: Sony Music Entertainment. (1999)

Hokusai, K. (1830). *Thirty-six Views of Mount Fuji: The Great Wave off Kanagawa* [Color
 wood-block print]. Honolulu, HI: Honolulu Academy of Arts.

Joplin, S. (1902). The entertainer [Recorded by R. Eaton]. On *Joplin Piano Rags* [CD]. New
 York: Sony Music Entertainment. (2002)

McLean, D. (1980). Vincent. On *American pie* [CD]. Hollywood, CA: Liberty Records.

Quinn, J. (1997). *Deaf* [Glazed terra cotta]. Private collection.

Schramm, S. (1993). *Pacific blue* [Cassette]. Three Lakes, WI: NorthSound.

van Gogh, V. (1889). *La meridienne (d'apres millet)* [Oil on canvas]. Paris: Musée d'Orsay.

Walela, C. (1996). The Apache honoring song. On *Tribal voices* [Cassette]. Redway, CA:
 EarthBeat! Records.

Index

Page references followed by *f* indicate figures.